The Little
Green
Book

365 WAYS TO LOVE THE PLANET

CRE▲TIVE
HOMEOWNER®

The Little Green Book

365 WAYS TO LOVE THE PLANET

BY JOE PROVEY AND OWEN LOCKWOOD

CREATIVE HOMEOWNER®, Upper Saddle River, New Jersey

The Little Green Book: 365 Ways to Love the Planet
Produced by Home & Garden Editorial Services
Project Manager: Joe Provey
Contributors: Nicholas Day, Marina Marchesi,
    Corinna Provey, Jill Schoff
Design: Horst Weber
Layout: Venera Alexandrova
Photo Research: MaryAnn Kopp
Copy Editor: Owen Lockwood
Editorial Assistant: MaryAnn Kopp
Front Cover Photography: courtesy of NASA/Visible Earth
Back Cover Photography: *top* iStockphoto.com/Carmen
    Martinez, *middle* iStockphoto.com/Todd Arbini,
    bottom left Joseph Provey *bottom center* iStock-
    photo.com/Dr. Heinz Linke *bottom right* iStock-
    photo.com/Josh Webb

Creative Homeowner
VP, Publisher: Timothy O. Bakke
Production Director: Kimberly H. Vivas
Art Director: David Geer
Managing Editor: Fran Donegan
Photo Coordinator: Robyn Poplasky
Junior Editor: Jennifer Calvert
Digital Imaging Specialist: Frank Dyer

Manufactured in the United States of America

Current Printing (last digit)
10 9 8 7 6 5 4 3 2 1

The Little Green Book: 365 Ways to Love the Planet,
    First Edition
Library of Congress Control Number: 2008921440
ISBN-10: 1-58011-418-0
ISBN-13: 978-1-58011-418-9

CREATIVE HOMEOWNER®
A Division of Federal Marketing Corp.
24 Park Way
Upper Saddle River, NJ 07458
www.creativehomeowner.com

Planet Friendly Publishing
✔ Made in the United States
✔ Printed on Recycled Paper

GREEN EDITION Learn more at www.greenedition.org

At Creative Homeowner we're committed to producing books in an earth-friendly manner and to helping our customers make greener choices.

Manufacturing books in the United States ensures compliance with strict environmental laws and eliminates the need for international freight shipping, a major contributor to global air pollution.

And printing on recycled paper helps minimize our consumption of trees, water, and fossil fuels. *The Little Green Book* was printed on paper made with 10% post-consumer waste. According to Environmental Defense's Paper Calculator, by using this innovative paper instead of conventional papers, we achieved the following environmental benefits:

Trees Saved: 33

Water Saved: 11,954 gallons

Solid Waste Eliminated: 1,978 pounds

Air Emissions Eliminated: 3,647 pounds

For more information on our environmental practices, please visit us online at www.creativehomeowner.com/green

Dedication

To today's generation of young adults that has breathed new life into the green movement of their parents—and to all the generations that follow.

Acknowledgments

We would like to thank our editor on this project, Fran Donegan, for suggesting the idea for this book and for his helpful suggestions throughout its creation. We would also like to thank Creative Homeowner Art Director David Geer for his helpful guidance in regard to the book's design.

contents

Small changes in the way we live, multiplied by a large number of citizens, can have a huge impact on the environment. If we all turned our roofs into solar collectors, wars over oil would cease. If we walked more or took mass transit, we'd all breath easier. If we ate sustainably produced foods, we'd help eliminate pollution and world starvation. If we became smarter consumers, we'd reduce waste. If we taught our children to be green, we'd watch as the next generation creates new solutions. Read through our "365 ways" and see how many you can implement.

Left: Beehives located in an orchard.

CHAPTER 1

Eating Friendly

What we choose to eat has, of course, a direct effect on our health. But it also can affect the environment and how well people eat in the rest of the world. So get started. Adopt a greener diet by eating organic and responsibly produced foods now.

CONTENTS

EAT MORE VEGGIES

1

You don't have to go vegetarian. (We're not.) But even committed carnivores should know that cutting down on meat can help the environment. That's because meat production is—let's face it—really inefficient, especially when you factor in all the land, water, and chemicals that are required for animal feed. The runoff from fertilizers for animal feed is believed to be the world's largest source of water pollution. And because livestock release methane and nitrous oxide—greenhouse gases that are more powerful than carbon dioxide—it's responsible for almost 20 percent of total greenhouse gas emissions. That's more than all forms of transportation combined.

Sadly, these figures may worsen. Worldwide meat consumption is estimated to double by 2050. Of course, buying local and sustainably raised meat, which you should do, can solve a few of these problems. But an occasional day without a hamburger will solve even more. For guidance, see Madhur Jaffrey's delectable cookbook, *World Vegetarian*.

2 MADE IN THE SHADE

Most coffee is grown with potent chemicals on land that's been deforested. Choosing shade-grown coffee challenges that system. It's the traditional method of coffee production: farmers plant coffee trees underneath the forest's canopy. That preserves the biodiversity of the surrounding habitat. Many shade-grown coffees are often called bird-friendly because shady coffee plantations are precious way stations for migrating birds. Look for coffee that's certified by the Smithsonian or the Rainforest Alliance. Also, small-scale artisanal coffee roasters often buy coffee that's grown sustainably; ask your roaster for details.

Think about where the beans come from the next time you're sipping your favorite brew.

3 SUBSCRIBE TO A CSA

A CSA, which stands for community supported agriculture, is a simple but brilliant concept: a farm sells shares in its future crops to subscribers, who receive a box of produce every week. The details vary from CSA to CSA—how long a subscription lasts, what and how much people receive, how the box gets delivered—but the model stays the same. It gives people in cities a stake in what's happening in the countryside.

CSA members pay in advance, which means they share the risk of farming. For example, if a flood wipes out the squash field, then no one gets any squash that year. It's very rare that a farm suffers a truly catastrophic event, but if it happens, the up-front payments provide farmers with a guarantee that they'll survive. In fact, when a few CSA farms have lost crops in the past their subscribers have stayed with them the following year. It's that sense of community that makes CSAs uniquely valuable. To find a CSA in your area, see localharvest.org.

4 SUPPORT LOCAL FARMS

The local food revolution is here. With farmers' markets multiplying across the country, it is easier to eat local than ever before. So why should you? Here's a selfish reason: taste. Local produce is much fresher than what's at the supermarket, where the average fruit or vegetable has traveled 1,500 miles. Buying locally means you're cutting down on 1,500 miles worth of carbon emissions, too. Plus, small farmers often grow delicious varieties that have been abandoned by industrial agriculture; choosing them boosts genetic diversity.

But there's a simpler reason to buy local: it preserves farms as part of your local landscape. Farmland is disappearing by the millions of acres every year. By supporting local farmers, you're voting for open spaces instead of strip malls. Making a meal from a farmers' market connects you to your community. For additional information about eating locally, see localharvest.org.

Farmers' markets, a fixture of many cities around the world, have made a comeback in the United States. Check for dates and times in your area.

5 SHUCK AN OYSTER

Aquaculture, or fish farming, often wastes more fish than it produces. (See "Vegetarian-Fed Fish" on page 18.) But oyster farming is aquaculture at its best. Oysters, which are raised in suspended bags or on the seafloor in shallow water, not only don't damage their environment, they actually restore it. By filtering 50 gallons of water a day, an adult oyster simultaneously feeds itself and purifies the water around it. In fact, in many coastal communities, farmed oysters have helped establish a healthy ecosystem, and other species have followed in their filtered wake.

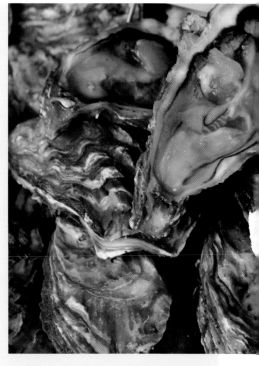

Avoid oysters in the months without r's, when the bivalves are spawning. They're at their best in the fall and winter. And if you live near a coast, support the regional economy by eating local. For more information on North American oysters—where to find them and how to shuck them—see Rowan Jacobsen's *A Geography of Oysters: The Connoisseur's Guide to Oyster Eating in North America.*

6 COOK THE KIDNEYS

As butchers know, eating only the choice cuts is a waste. For example, steaks make up only a tiny percentage of a cow. That's why a responsible carnivore should commit to eating the less popular parts, too. Happily, that's not a chore. Few dishes beat a roast that's cooked slow and low, and even much-maligned offal, such as kidneys and sweetbreads, is delicious when prepared correctly. Honest. For recipes and more information about nose-to-hoof cooking, see Hugh Fearnley-Whittingstall's *The River Cottage Meat Book.*

7 BUY A MEAT SHARE

It's still tough to find sustainably raised meat. The steak at your local supermarket almost certainly comes from vast and polluting feedlots. If you want to always have reliable meat around, you'll have to source it yourself. The best and cheapest way to do that is to buy a share of an animal from organic farmers, many of whom will sell their cows or pigs in halves, quarters, or even smaller sizes.

This might sound like a hassle because you'll need a freezer and you'll have to think ahead. If, say, you want a pork loin tomorrow, you'll need to know that tonight. But if you adjust to those complications, this is the perfect system. You know exactly where your meat comes from, and because there's no middleman, both you and the farmer come out with more money. For smaller quantities at a time, look for a local meat CSA, a new variation on the traditional CSA concept. (See "Subscribe to a CSA" on page 12.) See eatwild.com for local suppliers.

Small fish are typically less expensive than big fish and are just as tasty. They are also often better for you and more likely to have been harvested in a sustainable manner.

8 EAT THE SMALL FRY

When you're at the fishmonger, leave the larger fish—the tuna, the swordfish, the cod—in the case and look at the small fish: sardines, anchovies, and smelts. These fish are more fecund and abundant, which means their stocks are healthy. And although they're often overlooked, they make for great eating, especially when grilled. The "buy small" rule includes mussels, clams, and oysters, all of which are farmed sustainably.

Organic eggs generally come from better-cared-for hens, are better for you, and are less likely to be a cause of water and air pollution.

9 BUY CAGE-FREE EGGS

Put down those 99-cent eggs. The only way to produce eggs that cheaply is to cram hens in tiny wire, or battery, cages. The waste from the hens, who can hardly move, drops onto the cages beneath. That massive amount of waste—think 80,000 hens in a single operation—is responsible for significant water and air pollution. Until recently, 300 million hens laid eggs in battery cages each year, but many consumers and restaurants are now opting for cage-free eggs instead. The European Union is even phasing out all battery cages by 2012.

Cage-free eggs aren't ideal. The term itself is unregulated and unverified, although it usually refers to crowding laying hens on the floor of a large barn. That's more humane than a battery cage, of course, and it reduces the density of waste. However, organic eggs are even better because they almost always come from smaller flocks.

10 CARRY A CHEAT SHEET

Eating fish has become very complicated. For example, wild arctic char is okay, but farmed arctic char isn't. And is it Pacific or Atlantic halibut that's sustainably fished? It's too much information to keep in your head. Luckily, several nonprofits publish sustainable seafood wallet cards, which list best, acceptable, and bad choices. The cards are regularly updated, and more information is available on each organization's Web site. Our favorites are published by the Monterey Bay Aquarium (mbayaq.org) and the Blue Ocean Institute (blueocean.org).

11 THE SKINNY ON TUNA

Canned tuna, a high-quality convenience food, isn't any less convenient to buy in its sustainable form. Look for cans labeled troll, pole, or handline-caught. These are fishing methods that dramatically reduce bycatch, the term for unwanted fish that are accidentally caught. (Conventional tuna fishing kills high numbers of turtles, sharks, and many other species.) Canned tuna is largely from skipjack, yellowfin, or albacore, all of which reproduce rapidly and have relatively healthy stocks. (And if you ever see bluefin tuna in a sushi restaurant, shun it because the species has been decimated.)

If you're wondering about mercury, you're safe with these recommendations. Mercury levels rise alongside size, and because these tunas are smaller, they haven't accumulated significant mercury levels. Albacore tuna can be high in mercury, but the low-tech fishing methods above generally catch the smaller albacore, which have far lower levels. (Tuna that's called solid white is albacore. Pregnant women should still limit their consumption.)

When buying wild salmon, look for the Marine Stewardship Council seal. It certifies that the salmon comes from sustainable, monitored fisheries.

12 CHOOSE WILD SALMON

We've cautioned you about farmed salmon. (See page 18.) But here's the good news: you can eat Alaskan wild salmon. That might seem paradoxical—aren't wild fish more endangered than farmed?—but the Alaskan salmon fishery is exceptionally well managed and is a model for other fisheries. Its fish carry the seal of the Marine Stewardship Council, a nonprofit organization that certifies sustainable fisheries. Look for the blue MSC logo.

13 VEGETARIAN-FED FISH

Unfortunately, that cheap salmon fillet in the supermarket really is too good to be true. Farmed fish such as salmon are raised inside open pens in coastal waters, so whatever's in the pens ultimately winds up in the surrounding environment. The waste from the densely packed pens is deeply damaging to other species; the antibiotics falling from the pens don't help either. Fish that escape often breed with wild fish, causing genetic pollution. And farms use massive quantities of small, wild-caught fish to feed carnivorous fish. Estimates vary, but it takes at least several pounds of wild fish to make a pound of farmed salmon. (There are more sustainable salmon farms, but currently there aren't labels to distinguish them. Turn to page 17 to see why you should buy wild salmon.)

Instead of farmed carnivorous fish, look for domestic vegetarian fish such as catfish, rainbow trout, or tilapia. Their diet doesn't decimate wild populations, and they're raised inland, where any pollution they create is contained and treated.

14 REDUCE FOOD WASTE

Surprisingly, throwing out food might be worse for the environment than tossing, say, plastic. That's because when food decomposes, it releases methane, a powerful greenhouse gas that's 25 times as potent as CO_2. And Americans throw out 25 million tons of food each year—a quarter of all the food we buy, according to the USDA. Break the cycle by planning ahead. Go to the grocery store with a menu in mind. Factor in leftovers, and if you freeze anything, keep a list of what's frozen on the outside of the freezer.

15 AND THE WINNER IS...

The most sustainable backyard pet isn't a dog or a cat—it's a chicken.

We're serious. Chickens will catch garden pests, control weeds, turn leftovers into fertilizer, and—here's the exciting part—produce a copious number of fresh, shockingly good eggs , with more key vitamins and less cholesterol and saturated fat. And chickens that aren't cooped up in cages are, somewhat surprisingly, smart and highly entertaining, especially old-time heritage strains that haven't been bred for confinement and that lay delightfully multicolored eggs. Chickens are also easy to make happy and, no, they're not noisy—but roosters are, which is why cities often ban them.

Driven by the "eat local" movement, the number of backyard poultry believers is expanding exponentially. Look into local regulations; they may require coops to be a certain distance from houses or they may limit the number of chickens. The essential resource is *Backyard Poultry* magazine, or backyardpoultrymag.com.

Want to raise chickens? Check out **Backyard Poultry** *magazine (backyardpoultrymag.com).*

16 SHUN FACTORY PORK

How do we say this? Pigs go to the bathroom a whole lot, which is why industrial hog farming—antibiotic-dosed pigs crammed tightly inside a barn—produces jaw-dropping quantities of waste. It's a well-documented source of water and air pollution. The biggest environmental spill in American history occurred when a North Carolina manure lagoon—the industry term for a pond of excrement—spilled 25.8 million gallons of toxic sludge. Say no to Smithfield, the world's largest pork processor, and support small pork producers instead.

17 BUY HAPPY, NOT MAD

Almost every meat eater knows these terrifying words: mad cow. Formally known as bovine spongiform encephalopathy, or BSE, mad cow is a fatal neurological disease that eats away at the spinal cord and brain of cattle. The BSE-epidemic began in Britain in the late 1980s, and the first BSE-infected cow was found in the United States in 2003. It's widely believed that humans who eat beef from BSE-infected cattle can develop a variant of the devastating Creutzfeldt-Jakob disease, which has killed at least 165 people in Britain.

Here's the good news: you can cut your risk down to virtually zero. Scientists now agree that cows originally acquired BSE by eating cows—they were fed grain that included, as a protein boost, the unwanted parts of slaughtered cattle. That cannibalistic practice is now banned in the United States, but giving that feed to other animals—potential protein sources for future cattle feed—isn't.

Instead of worrying over mad cow, buy organic, or grass-fed, vegetarian beef, which should be safe—it will taste better and be better for you than mass-produced beef. See eatwild.com.

18 WORST-RANKED PRODUCE

There's a surprising range in the amount of pesticides used on nonorganic fruits and vegetables. And because organic produce isn't always available, or affordable, it helps to know what's safe to buy. The nonprofit Environmental Working Group (EWG) recently did a study that ranked 45 fruits and vegetables by their pesticide content. Here are the five safest: onions, avocados, frozen sweet corn, pineapples, and mangoes. And the five with the highest residues are as follows: peaches, apples, sweet peppers, celery, and nectarines. For a pesticide wallet guide from the EWG, go to foodnews.org/walletguide.php.

19 HORMONE-FREE MILK

There's been a lot of attention recently focused on an obscure hormone for dairy cows called rBST. Manufactured by Monsanto, a biotech company, and approved by the FDA, the hormone became popular with the dairy industry because it increases a cow's milk production. But the stress of increased milking has been known to make cows sick, and many observers worry that the hormone might be even worse for us.

Hormones in dairy products may pose serious reproductive problems and possibly an increased risk of cancer. It's worth noting that the FDA is almost alone in its conviction that rBST is safe; the hormone's never been approved for use in Europe or Canada. Eliminating it from your diet is easy, though. All organic milk is free of rBST, and many dairy companies, aware of increased public concern, are now marketing hormone-free milk, mentioning it prominently on the label.

Help to keep cows from being overworked! Only buy organic milk.

"*You must love the crust of the earth on which you dwell more than the sweet crust of any bread or cake; you must be able to extract nutriment out of a sand heap.*"
— *Henry David Thoreau*

 20 ### STORE FOOD SAFELY

We're not talking about roaches. By safely, we mean phthalate free, and by phthalates, we mean a class of chemicals that is used in perfumes, solvents, and plastics, especially PVC. Phthalates are what soften and mold plastics. Unfortunately, heat and repeated use can leach those chemicals, and phthalates have been linked to a variety of serious health problems in animals and people. Studies have shown that exposure to phthalates has altered hormones and reproductive systems.

Because phthalates don't build up in the body, if you switch to phthalate-free products, the chemicals will be flushed out. So what is phthalate free? Well, good old glass. You can freeze and store food in glass canning containers. Use a drinking glass at work or switch to a stainless-steel water bottle. Among plastics, go with polyethylene-based products such as Nalgene.

An easy way to tell plastics apart is by the recycling code: number 3 plastics contain phthalates. It's safest to go with glass (shown).

21 START A FOOD CO-OP

Food co-ops are often considered cultural holdovers from the 1960s, the sort of stores that carried brown rice and honey, and not much else. In fact, cooperative groceries are still a vital part of the sustainable food landscape and, fortunately, they're not going away. Co-ops give people a voice in their community; they're democratic, neighborhood-building institutions. Because they're smaller and more nimble, co-ops can work closely with local farmers to source, say, a crop of potatoes or a couple of lambs—the sort of reliable purchases that small farmers depend on. And co-op members can make sure that everything in the store meets their standards: nontoxic, fair trade, minimally processed. You might say that food co-ops have never been more relevant.

Want to set up a food co-op? See the manual How to Start a Food Co-op *at cgin.coop.*

22 DINE WITH FRIENDS

Establish a regular, environmentally friendly dinner party with friends. Make it a formal dinner or a potluck or a rotating event—that doesn't matter. What matters is building that all-important sense of a like-minded community—a community that cares about what happens to the wider world. Together you'll come up with countless new ideas and resources for living greener.

23 STAY FRESHER LONGER

An astounding quantity of food waste comes from fruits and vegetables simply going bad. That's because decomposition releases methane, a greenhouse gas that's a contributor to global warming. Learn how to store fresh produce properly—it isn't intuitive. Eggplants, for example, should be stored in the crisper, but tomatoes never should. Onions are okay at room temperature, but not potatoes. For the best advice on how to find and keep the best fruits and vegetables—and for excellent recipes for using them—see Russ Parsons' *How to Pick a Peach*.

24 BUY IN SEASON

Let's face it: tomatoes always taste best in August. Eating food in season is a conscious act that brings you closer to the environment, including the farms in your region because in-season food is more likely to be grown locally. Local and seasonal food isn't "force grown" with fertilizers, which leads to nitrogen pollution, and it'll be better for you, too. Produce that isn't trucked across the country is more likely to ripen on the plant, which increases its nutritional value. And even in the cold months, delicious, frost-sweetened hearty greens and root crops can be found.

25 PICK YOUR OWN FRUIT

There's no shortage of eco-minded reasons to pick your own fruit: supporting a local farm and the local economy; cutting down on packaging; helping to maintain a diverse landscape. But we'd like to list a few selfish reasons, too. In order to survive shipment, fruit is conventionally picked way before it becomes ripe. So when you're at an orchard, twisting a soft peach off a tree, you're getting a taste that's been bred out of the industrial food system. And here's another reason: there are few things more beautiful than a row of bleeding-red raspberry bushes or a line of trees that are heavy with apples or peaches.

When you get home and wonder what you're going to do with it all, remember the wonder of homemade jam. (See "Now We're Jamming" on page 31.)

Treat yourself by visiting a nearby orchard or berry farm during harvest time.

26 PACK A LUNCH

Picking up a quick lunch to go while at work inadvertently produces an astounding amount of waste. The bags, the individual wrappers, the napkins, the plastic utensils are all used once and then trashed. Here's an eco-conscious alternative: bring your own. You'll get to control what you're eating and what you're tossing. Pack reusable utensils, cloth napkins, and a cloth lunch bag or—wait for it—a lunch box. (You don't have to get one with cartoon characters.)

If you have children in school, packing their lunch has environmental benefits beyond reducing waste. It means opting out of the polluting industrial agriculture complex that's propping up the national school lunch program— huge quantities of factory farmed meat, for example, are purchased by the government and donated to schools. For more information on reducing waste, see wastefreelunches.org. For more info on healthy school lunches, see lunchlessons.org.

27 GO BACK TO WAX PAPER

Plastic storage bags have lured us away from their more sustainable predecessors: wax paper and the waxed-paper bag. Unlike plastic bags, most will naturally biodegrade. But if you continue using plastic bags, remember to reuse them. Hammer in a few nails next to the dish drainer for easy drying. For eco-friendly unbleached waxed-paper bags, look for the Natural Value line.

28 CUT OUT DISPOSABLES

After a party, the amount of trash can be daunting. Recycling isn't the solution. If you've used paper plates, they're only recyclable if absolutely clean. But even if you'd prefer not to use glass or ceramic, switching from paper plates and plastic glasses and utensils is simple. Look for reusable plastic items with environmentally friendly numbers. (See page 22.) And if you really want something to toss, buy products that are either labeled compostable—they'll break down faster—or made from recycled materials.

29 CHURN YOUR OWN

Here's what the premium ice cream companies don't want you to know: with a low-cost ice cream maker, you can make better ice cream than you can buy in any supermarket. There's no catch. In exchange for cutting down on packaging (and cost), you'll get fresh ice cream that's gloriously rich. Ice cream makers are available for around $50. For a lifetime's worth of recipes, see David Lebovitz's *The Perfect Scoop*.

30 FILTER YOUR OWN WATER

Filtering your own water is certainly a lot easier than lugging home jugs of bottled water. But first you'll have to find out what's in your water. That's easy. The Environmental Protection Agency requires cities to disclose exactly what comes out of municipal faucets. These documents are called Consumer Confidence Reports, or CCRs, and are often available on city Web sites. The magazine *Consumer Reports* recently analyzed the CCRs of the 25 largest cities and found that only three could claim zero water-quality violations.

There are a mind-numbing number of filter options out there. For most water systems, a faucet or countertop filter, which addresses smell and taste issues, will be adequate. But systems with more serious contaminants—and if your house was built before 1986, it may have pipes that are soldered with lead—require more advanced technologies. Look for whole-house reverse osmosis systems.

31 A SIMPLE SOUP STOCK

With a little bit of planning, you'll never need to buy stock or broth again. Here's how to become self-sufficient: when trimming vegetables, put what's left over in a container in the freezer. Add extra vegetables when you have them—and don't worry if they're only peels or ends. If you roast a chicken, freeze the carcass; if you have a bone-in roast, set aside the bones. And on a gray day, throw it all in a stockpot (make sure there are some carrots and onions); cover it with cold water; and then let the pot gently bubble for a few hours.

32 BREAST-FEED IF POSSIBLE

Most of what's said about breast feeding focuses on its health benefits. It's rarely mentioned that breast feeding is clearly the environmentally preferable choice, too. There's no plastic or paper waste, no energy expended in production, no land devoted to growing feed crops.

Of course, breast feeding isn't always possible, and what's most important is having a well-nourished baby. Thankfully, there are an increasing number of organic formula brands on the market.

> "*The act of putting into your mouth what the earth has grown is perhaps your most direct interaction with the earth.*"
> — Frances Moore Lappe

33 HOMEMADE BABY FOOD

There's no need to feed a baby anything with sugar, salt, additives, or preservatives. Unfortunately, that's what you're getting when you open a jar of just about any brand of baby food. Stop spraining your wrists and start puréeing your own baby mush instead. Cook vegetables or fruits just until they're soft. (Steaming works well because the less cooking, the more vitamins and minerals are preserved.) Then add water or milk to thin the purée, and pour it in ice cube trays. When frozen, pop out the cubes and put them in freezer bags. (Vegetables and fruit will last at least half a year; meat should be eaten sooner.)

You can also use an inexpensive, hand-cranked food mill to purée whatever you've cooked up for your own dinner. Until babies grow up and start developing preferences, they can be thankfully, if temporarily, easy to feed. Don't add salt or sugar—babies don't need either—and remember that you're not the person tasting it.

Making wine from local grape harvests is a tradition, thousands of years old, that will keep you in touch with the seasons and the soil—and save you buckets of money, too.

34 A REAL HOUSE WINE

Even though winemaking isn't just for Italian grandfathers, the low-input, no-waste craft is somehow always over-looked. But with a couple of jugs and a starter kit—forget the grapes; there's perfectly good grape concentrate of countless varieties—it isn't much more complicated than baking bread. And, yes, if you follow directions and keep everything clean—bacteria is the buga-boo of winemakers—we promise that it'll be highly, highly potable.

35 FREEZE MEATS PROPERLY

Because finding sustainably produced meat can be a challenge, we recommend using your freezer to keep what you do find. It's particularly important, therefore, to keep meat safe from the flavor-sucking power of freezer burn.

Most meat will keep six months in a freezer bag. Just before sealing the bag, push out, or suck out with a straw, the excess air. For the best storage, vacuum pack it. Vacuum sealers are flawless and reasonably priced. Their minor environmental impact is far less substantial than buying a new cut of meat.

Making and canning your own jam (or vegetables) isn't as difficult as you may believe. An online search will come up with mail-order suppliers. We like canningpantry.com.

36 NOW WE'RE JAMMING

If making your own jams and preserves sounds too old-school—something your grandmother did—a spoonful of a fresh strawberry conserve will change your mind. A good homemade jam is an altogether different product than what's sold in stores. That's because you can reduce the quantity of sugar so the essence of the fruit shines through, and you can use fresh, locally grown fruit that's at its peak of ripeness. A summer day spent picking berries and preserving them is topped only by the winter day when you open up the jar.

You'll hear that making your own jam is difficult or dangerous. But with the right equipment, it's neither. It is, however, immediately rewarding. For ideas, see *The Jamlady Cookbook* by Beverly Ellen Schoonmaker Alfeld.

37 BREW YOUR OWN BEER

The craft-brew revolution came out of the basements of home brewers, and if you've got any do-it-yourself inclinations, your beer can be as good as anything in the walk-in cooler. The only real requirement is patience. With minimal input—equipment that's similar to that used for making wine (see page 30) and a few ingredients sold in home-brew stores—you've got an almost renewable resource. You can even reuse old beer bottles; that's a form of recycling with immediate rewards.

38 FIND A REGIONAL WINERY

Even hard-core "eat local" diets usually exclude a few things: coffee, olive oil, wine. Scratch that last item off the list. In the last decade the number of wineries in the United States has doubled to almost 5,000; there's a winery (right) in every state, including, yes, Alaska. Michigan's Riesling is unmatched in the United States. Virginia's wines from the Viognier grape may be the best outside of France. And uncorking a regional wine comes with all the ecological benefits of buying local. For more information, see winesandtimes.com.

Cast-iron cookware is a safe, inexpensive, and smart way to cook. It will last forever if you rub it down with vegetable oil regularly and avoid letting it sit in water for long periods.

39 STICK TO SAFE COOKWARE

After reports that some nonstick cookware might be a carcinogen that enters the bloodstream, all cookware has begun to seem a little scary. Here's a primer: cast iron is a tried-and-true material that can even improve your health (by getting more iron in your diet). Stainless steel and glass are perfectly safe. Copper conducts heat wonderfully but is wildly expensive and has to be immaculately lined with other metals; traces of copper can make you ill. Aluminum is more complicated. Cookware that's lined with aluminum is still illegal in much of Europe—acidic foods can leach out tiny amounts of it. Any high-quality aluminum cookware will be anodized, a chemical process that seals in the aluminum impenetrably. If that makes you nervous, go with cast iron and stainless steel. Instead of buying the new and theoretically safe nonstick pans, try this: heat up an empty pan and only add oil or butter after the pan's hot. The dry heat will close up microscopic scratches, creating an effectively nonstick surface.

40 ORGANIC RESTAURANTS

There are very few officially organic restaurants in the United States. Certification procedures are awkward and time-consuming, and few have bothered. But more owners and chefs than ever before are purchasing organic, locally grown vegetables and meats. They're even putting the names of the farms where they buy on their menus. When you go out to dine, ask the chef or the waiter if the restaurant buys local and organic. Support those who do.

Can't get there in person? Go online and order an organic restaurant's cookbook. Most have them. Our favorite is *The Best of Bloodroot* from the Bridgeport, Connecticut, restaurant of the same name.

41 ORGANIC LINENS

Even if you've eliminated food grown with pesticides and chemical fertilizers, there's a good chance your wholesome dinner is sitting on something that was dosed with both of those things.

We're talking about your tablecloth. Cotton production is extremely toxic, consuming large quantities of potent, polluting chemicals, and vinyl coverings aren't any better. So look for tablecloths made from organic cotton or organic linen, which create none of those problems.

42 COOK WITH THE SUN

If you enjoy cooking outside, make room for a solar cooker in your outdoor kitchen. It takes a bit more patience to cook a meal on a solar cooker, but it will reduce your use of fossil fuels and greenhouse gas output, and is smoke and flame free. It will also teach your kids a lot about the power and the overall potential of the sun. There are many types of solar cookers, including kettles, ovens, and grills. While the latter will probably not replace your charcoal or gas-fired barbecue, you can use it to sauté vegetables, scramble eggs, and panfry burgers.

Solar ovens come in many sizes and types. Typically, reflectors must be adjusted to reflect sunlight onto the cooking chamber. This Sun BD Corporation unit (sunbdcorp.com) reaches 300 degrees F and has a thermostatically-controlled electrical element that automatically switches on when clouds roll by—and off again when the sun returns.

43 BE AN EFFICIENT COOK

In the kitchen, we waste gas and electricity every day without even realizing it. Being an energy-efficient cook means just paying attention. Cover your pots with lids so the steam heat stays in. Use large pans on large burners and small pans on small burners; otherwise, much of the heat dissipates. Dig out your pressure cooker, which can cut energy use by 50 percent. Check your oven temperature, and bake with glass or ceramic pans, which do the work of metal pans at 25 degrees cooler. Only preheat the oven when necessary, and harness the oven's heat to cook many things at once—the heat's already there, after all. If your oven has a self-cleaning function, only use it sporadically because the high temperature sucks up energy. And if you're making something small, dispense with the oven altogether: pick up a pint-sized, energy-efficient toaster oven.

44 CRACK OPEN A LOCAL ONE

Thirty years ago, the only American breweries were corporate behemoths making weak, homogenous beers. That's hard to believe, given the glorious diversity on shelves today, but it is evidence that microbreweries, which strengthen local economies and identities, can't be taken for granted.

These craft breweries are often at the forefront of sustainable business practices. Small in size and focused locally, not nationally, many are also experimenting with renewable technologies, working to reduce transportation pollution and packaging waste, and often buying locally produced ingredients. Many have also unveiled all-organic lines. But craft beers will always be up against multinationals with more advertising, better distribution, and lower price tags. So remember: when you're buying local beer, you're supporting an ethic, not just a brand. For more on sustainable breweries, see *Fermenting Revolution: How to Drink Beer and Save the World* by Christopher O'Brien.

CHAPTER 2

Conserving Energy

Discovering a source of clean, renewable, safe, and cheap energy will transform mankind. But while we're waiting for that miracle to come, the best thing we can do is to conserve what we have by not using so much. Here are some ways to get started.

CONTENTS

BEEF UP INSULATION

45

You don't see it, but it's there, keeping your heating and cooling bills low and improving your comfort level. We're talking about insulation. Making sure your home is properly and adequately insulated is one of the best ways to prevent heat from flowing into or out of your home. Do you have enough insulation in your ceiling/attic, walls, and basement? Millions of homes do not, and they're wasting energy. Consider adding insulation where it already exists and installing insulation in places that don't have it but should, such as crawl spaces.

Contact a contractor or do some research to find out what insulation is best for your climate. Insulation effectiveness is measured in R-value, which indicates the resistance to heat flow. Northern regions generally require a higher R-value than Southern areas. According to the Department of Energy, a great insulation level for a ceiling or attic is R-45 in the North and R-38 in the South. For walls, it's R-23 in the North and R-19 in the South. When choosing a type of insulation, exercise caution because many insulation products—including some brands of fiberglass—contain formaldehyde.

46 HOME OFFICE GREEN-UP

Working from home? Great. You're already saving energy and resources by not driving to work. But you could be saving more. Don't heat or cool the entire house—do only what's necessary to be comfortable in your home office. In the winter, an extra sweater and a space heater should suffice. In the summer, a small fan or an open window will do the trick. Don't light the entire house either. A single desk lamp with an energy-efficient compact fluorescent bulb is often enough. Or better yet, rearrange furniture to take advantage of natural light. Use an Energy Star computer, and consider going with a laptop, which uses much less power than a desktop. Put the computer to sleep mode, and turn it off at the end of each day. See "Compute Using Less Energy" on page 55 for more tips.

Make use of natural light wherever possible. Use shades and blinds to control it.

47 DEFROST REGULARLY

Frost-free and self-defrost refrigerators use twice as much energy as manual-defrost models. If you go with the latter, defrost it periodically. Otherwise, water vapor condenses on the cooling coils over time, and the frost buildup reduces cooling efficiency—thus more energy is required to keep the motor running. Don't allow frost to build up more than $1/4$ inch in the fridge or freezer cabinet. If it does, turn off the power; remove all food; and allow the frost to melt with the door open. Don't scrape off the frost. When defrosted, clean the box and reset the thermostat.

48 BUY AN EFFICIENT AC

Believe it or not, people used to get by without air conditioning. They relied on shade, fans, and open windows. Nowadays, the humming of an air conditioner is omnipresent in the summer, with air conditioning accounting for about 15 percent of home energy use. If you must use an air conditioner to stay cool, make sure it's a high-efficiency unit. Room air conditioners are rated by their energy efficiency ratio (EER), which is the cooling capacity (in Btu/hour) divided by the input power (in watts). The higher the EER, the more efficient the AC is. The American Council for an Energy-Efficient Economy recommends an EER of at least 10.8.

Air conditioners with digital displays and built-in timers allow for better temperature control, which helps reduce energy usage. And look for a model with the Energy Star label—it exceeds federal standards by at least 10 percent. In the heat of the summer, a high-efficiency AC is too cool to pass up.

49 USE YOUR MICROWAVE

When warming up and cooking small amounts of food, use a microwave instead of a conventional oven. It will use about 50 percent less energy to do the job. The same goes for defrosting—although the most efficient method here, of course, is to plan ahead. For cooking large meals, however, the stove is usually more efficient. In the summer, using a microwave causes less heat in the kitchen, reducing the need for air conditioning.

According to BuyGreen, a source for green products, each minute spent driving to the mall uses 20 times more energy than a minute spent shopping online.

sixteenth of the energy of that used to operate a traditional retail store. Fewer trips to the store—in CO_2-emitting vehicles—also saves transportation energy. Still not convinced? Being an environmentally aware online shopper makes it easier to comparison shop, and you can often find Internet-only specials. Some sites offer free shipping, too.

50 SHOP ONLINE

Most people who shop online do so for the convenience. They can shop 24 hours a day—in their pajamas or even their "birthday suit," if they wish—and don't have to worry about crowded stores, long lines, and parking-spot searches. But avoiding these hassles may not be enough to keep you away from the mall. Well, shopping from home has its green benefits, too, particularly in energy savings. According to buygreen.com, a source for green products, e-commerce warehouses use one-

51 LOWER THE SETTING

Reduce the thermostat setting on your water heater to 120° F and save up to 10 percent of your hot water heating costs. You'll also slow mineral buildup and corrosion in your water heater and help it last longer. If you plan to be away from home for three days or longer, turn the thermostat down to its lowest setting or completely turn off the water heater. Look to your owner's manual for how to locate and operate the thermostat on your water heater.

If you have a dishwasher without a booster heater, it may require a water temperature between 130° and 140° F for optimum cleaning.

52 SLAY VAMPIRE POWER

Televisions, DVD players, computers, microwaves, coffeemakers, and other devices use electricity when they're off—it's known as phantom load or vampire power. Such appliances use up to 40 percent of their full power. To save this energy, use power strips and turn them off when you're not using the devices that are plugged into them. When the power strip is off, the attached appliances can no longer draw power from the outlet. The Smart Strip by BITS Limited automatically shuts off peripheral devices when the item plugged into the "control outlet" is turned off. The company claims the Smart Strip saves enough energy to pay for itself in 14 weeks on average. Be careful about using a power strip for items with clocks; they'll have to be reset each time the power strip is turned off. And, of course, don't use power strips for refrigerators and other items that need power 24/7.

In summer, use ceiling fans to stay cool. In winter, use them to move hot air that has accumulated near the ceiling to floor level—where you need it.

53 COOL USING FANS

Fans are the best way to keep cool. They work by causing perspiration on your skin to evaporate, allowing the skin to cool. Wearing lightweight, loose, absorbent clothing will help fans do their job better. And think how cool you'll feel knowing that by not using your AC, you're helping reduce global warming and ozone depletion—the twin horrors associated with the refrigerants used in most air-conditioning units. Refrigerants are being phased out over the next 20 years, but why wait? You can switch to fans anytime.

54 SAVE LIGHT AT NIGHT

Lighting up the yard at night for safety, security, and beauty makes sense, but wasting watts does not. Here are a few things you can do to reduce usage:

• **Use solar-powered** path lights or reflectors to mark driveways and walkways.

• **For security lighting,** use motion detectors and timers.

• **Use low-voltage fixtures** where possible.

Don't overdo it when it comes to security lighting. Low levels of light are just as effective as high levels—maybe more so.

• **Install energy-efficient lamps.**

• **Eliminate** any unnecessary lighting.

55 USE A HUMIDIFIER

A humidifier is good for the skin because it helps prevent dryness. It's also good for reducing energy usage. Indoor air tends to have very little moisture in colder months because of the use of furnaces and other heating devices. As a result, our body moisture evaporates quickly and we start to feel cold, so we turn up the thermostat. We don't have to. The additional moisture from a humidifier can increase the heat index, making 68° F feel like 76° F, according to the Department of Energy. Look for a model with a humidistat, which measures humidity levels and shuts off the unit when a desired level is reached. A model that automatically shuts off if the water runs dry is a good idea, too.

56 TURN OFF THE COFFEE

Instead of leaving your coffeemaker on to keep coffee warm, pour your fresh brew into a thermos. Or save the extra step by buying a model with an integrated insulated decanter the next time you need a new coffeemaker. You'll save energy—and your coffee will be better tasting, too.

57 CHECK AC FILTERS OFTEN

Keep your air conditioner from working harder than it has to by making sure to clean the filter frequently (or replace it frequently, if it's a disposable kind), especially during the summer. Filters should be cleaned monthly during the cooling season and once every other month the rest of the year. (You may need to clean or change it more frequently if you run the air conditioner constantly or if you have pets.) Doing so can save 5 percent of the energy used, because a dirty or clogged filter means the air conditioner must work harder and stay on longer to provide the same amount of cool air. Keep the cool air moving freely to keep your air conditioner running as efficiently as possible.

58 WORK OUT AND WARM UP

A daily workout is not only good for your waistline; it can also reduce your energy bill. Whether you jog, play a sport, or work out at the gym, regular exercise will elevate your body temperature and keep you feeling warmer for up to four hours. Conversely, a quick dip in the pool or a cool shower will lower your body temperature and reduce the need to rely on air conditioning.

Working out doesn't have to mean a drive to the gym or buying expensive home equipment. Practicing pilates, yoga, or good old-fashioned calisthenics at home will all do the trick.

59 USE CFLS (BUT CAREFULLY)

Compact fluorescent lights (CFLs) can have a significant impact on energy use at home and on the environment in general. Consider the fact that CFLs use about 75 percent less energy than standard incandescent

bulbs. That translates into a 12 percent savings on your electricity bill. In addition, they last up to 10 times longer than incandescent bulbs. Even more impressive, if every American home replaced just one light bulb with a CFL, we would save enough energy to light more than 3 million homes for a year and prevent greenhouse gases equivalent to the emissions of more than 800,000 cars.

CFLs are available in sizes and shapes for just about every type of lighting fixture, from table lamps to recessed lighting. Look for those that are Energy Star qualified. Install CFLs first in high-usage areas, such as kitchens and family rooms, where lights are typically left on for more than 15 minutes. (Switching CFLs on for shorter intervals will drastically reduce their life span.) Avoid placing them where they can easily be broken. CFLs, like other fluorescent bulbs, contain mercury, a poisonous heavy metal. CFLs also require special cleanup techniques should a bulb break, and they must be treated as hazardous waste when disposing of them.

If a compact fluorescent bulb breaks, open windows to allow mercury vapors to escape, and vacate the room. Clean up shards using gloves. Pick up small slivers with duct tape. Do not vacuum.

60 TANKLESS HOT WATER

Between 15 and 30 percent of the energy used for heating water is not used for laundry, bathing, dishwashing, or anything else. It's merely used for keeping the water hot while it's not being used. You can reduce this waste by insulating your hot water tank (see "Water Heater Blankets" on page 60) or by installing a tankless hot water heater. These units are compact, unlikely to ever fail and flood the basement, and supply continuous hot water at rates of about 4 to 7 gallons per minute, depending on how hot you need the water to be. Most units burn gas and cost $600 to $900.

"I'd put my money on the sun and solar energy. What a source of power! I hope we don't have to wait until oil and coal run out before we tackle that."
— Thomas Edison

61 SAVE FRIDGE ENERGY

Elsewhere in this book you can read about buying a new, efficient refrigerator. A new fridge is a major purchase that may not be in your budget. Fortunately, there are some things you can do to reduce the amount of energy your current fridge consumes. Try these energy-saving tips: **1.** Position it away from sources of heat, such as ovens, dishwashers, and sunny windows. **2.** Keep the coils clean. **3.** Replace seals that aren't tight. To check seals, close the door on a dollar bill. If the bill can be pulled out easily, the seal is not tight enough. **4.** Keep the temperature between 35° and 38° F. **5.** Know what's inside and where it's located, so you avoid those dreaded searches for just the right thing to eat—with door ajar and energy bills climbing.

Dim kitchen lights for dinners. It feels like candlelight and reduces energy usage at the same time. Dimmers are also ideal for dining rooms, bedrooms, hallways, and foyers.

62 USE DIMMER SWITCHES

The dim bulb is not so dim after all. Dimmer switches not only allow you to set the light level to match your mood or need, they save energy, too. Dim a light by 25 percent and save 20 percent of the watts needed to power it. As a bonus, lightbulbs will last up to 40 times longer on the dimmed setting. According to Lutron, a major maker of dimmer switches, an incandescent bulb will last 20 times longer if dimmed to 50 percent. Dimmable compact fluorescent bulbs, now available, also help save energy.

63 TURN OUT THE LIGHTS

A very simple thing, but so hard to remember. How many times have you woken up in the morning only to find that several lights were left burning all night long? Our very simple solution?

Write a polite note to the culprit. *"I turned off the lights for you last night."* Post it on their bedroom door, bathroom mirror, or cell phone. If you're the culprit, write yourself a note and post it where you're sure to see it before turning in for the evening.

64 MAINTAIN YOUR AC

Like furnaces, air conditioners lose efficiency—up to 5 percent per year—with each year of operation. You can stop this loss and keep your air conditioner within 95 percent of its original efficiency with regular servicing. The cost of such maintenance will quickly be recouped by reduced electric bills, fewer repairs, and longer life of the unit.

Be sure the serviceman checks the refrigerant level, along with the compressor, coils, motor, and belts. Low refrigerant will add significantly to the cost of operation. If your system is leaking, be sure to have the leak repaired—don't simply have more refrigerant added. Besides being against the law, the leak will do further damage to the Earth's protective ozone layer.

Air conditioners, despite being energy hogs, are sometimes a must. If you're going to use one, be responsible. Maintain it so it operates at peak efficiency and doesn't release coolant.

65 USE THE MOISTURE SENSOR

A moisture sensor shuts a dryer down when clothes are dry. An alternative to timers, it's available on most of today's dryers—and it's a feature you should be using. Doing so protects clothes, helps prevent dryer fires, and saves energy. A dryer uses a lot of energy—about 3.5 kWh for a full load per cycle. If you set your dryer on the moisture sensor, you can cut energy use by 15 percent. Using the moisture sensor may make your clothes last longer, too, because they won't be subject to over-drying.

66 LOWER THE THERMOSTAT

You've probably heard this one before. There's a reason why: it's a simple way to save energy and cut heating costs. According to the Department of Energy, you can save 1 to 3 percent on your heating bill for every degree you lower your thermostat. See how low you can go. Thermostats are often set unnecessarily to the upper 60s or low 70s. At night, sleep under a heavy blanket and see if you can handle the upper 50s. Some people go lower by using a bed warmer or electric blanket to get past the initial chill. The lower you set the thermostat, the more energy you'll save.

67 BUY GREEN POWER

Renewable energy, also known as green power, can generate electricity for your home. It refers to electricity supplied from renewable sources, such as wind, geothermal power, solar power, and hydropower. These renewable energy sources can

reduce the greenhouse-gas emissions and pollution from conventional sources of electricity generation, such as coal and nuclear plants. See if your current electricity provider offers, or plans to offer, the option of buying green power. (Most states have regulated utilities that offer green options.) If your company doesn't offer a green option and you live in a competitive-market area where there's a choice of suppliers, look for one that's committed to renewable energy. You'll pay a small premium (to cover the costs of purchasing or generating electricity from a green source), but isn't it worth it to know a portion of your power is derived from clean, renewable sources?

Sunrooms and sun porches can be custom-built or assembled from kits, above. Prefabricated units often come with intregal shades—a must for preventing overheating in summer.

68 GET A SOLAR BOOST

So your house was not designed to take advantage of the sun. That doesn't have to leave you out in the cold. There are plenty of things you can do to capture heat from the late fall to the early spring—and to prevent heat buildup in the summer.

If you have a sunroom or enclosed porch with a southern exposure, it can be used to collect tremendous amounts of heat. Use fans or natural convection to move air through a doorway from solar-warmed rooms to adjacent interior spaces. Just be sure to provide an opening for "return" air, such as a vent or an open window between the sunroom and the house, to ensure good air movement.

Even if you don't have a sunroom or sun porch, you can use blinds, shutters, drapes, or shades to control the sunlight entering rooms with southern exposures. Blinds are often the best choice because they can be adjusted to let light in (or to keep it out) while maintaining privacy. Drapes, however, offer a degree of insulation and may be better for areas with very cold winters.

69 USE STORM WINDOWS

Single-pane windows lose much more heat in winter than double-pane windows. But what can you do if you're not quite ready to replace all those single-pane windows with double-pane versions? If you live in a cold climate, you can spend less money and still save energy by using storm windows, which provide protection during inclement weather. Storm windows, which can be installed either inside or outside, improve energy efficiency by reducing air leakage and adding another layer of insulation to your home. They have other benefits as well; they reduce outside noise, minimize sun damage (to drapes, furniture, and so forth), and add an extra layer of home security.

70 INSTALL AN AWNING

Don't waste energy and money to cool your house when you can keep the heat out with a simple device: an awning. Awnings reduce the amount of sunlight that gets through glass doors and windows. This reduction in solar heat gain keeps your home's interior cooler on hot days—by as much as 8 to 15 degrees—which means your air conditioner doesn't have to run as long or as hard. In 2007, a study funded by the Professional Awning Manufacturers Association found that window awnings can reduce home cooling energy by as much as 26 percent in hot climates and 33 percent in cold climates.

Awning prices vary. A stationary window awning may cost a few hundred bucks while an electrically powered, retractable awning with wind and sun sensors can set you back thousands of dollars.

Awnings can increase a home's value by thousands of dollars. Their performance is affected by the style, the color of the fabric, and the exposure of the windows.

It's been estimated that drying a single load on a clothesline keeps between 3 and 4 pounds of carbon dioxide out of the atmosphere. Doing so regularly saves you about $75 per year on your energy bill.

71 DO LAUNDRY IN COLD WATER

The washing machine is one of the largest energy-consuming appliances in your home, and most of the energy is wasted heating the water. As much as 80 to 90 percent of the energy is used to heat the water, and the rest goes to powering the motor. Use cold water to wash your clothes whenever possible— you'll greatly reduce your energy consumption (up to 50 percent) and save big on your energy bill (hundreds of dollars a year). According to the Rocky Mountain Institute, washing with cold water instead of hot water uses 1,444 fewer kWh per year (based on a 39-gallon model doing 380 loads). And don't worry: many detergents work just fine in cold water. Always use a cold rinse, too.

72 DRY CLOTHES ON A LINE

Dryers account for a large amount of home energy use and carbon emissions. To be more environmentally friendly, try using a clothesline instead. Drying on a line can save 500 to 700 pounds of CO_2 a year. What could be better than using the most natural dryer of all, the sun? Your clothes—especially the elastics in socks and underwear—will last longer.

They'll smell fresher, too. And you won't mind those lower utility bills.

You don't have to give up your clothes dryer entirely, of course. Even if you hang your clothes out to line-dry once a week, or just during the summer, you'll still be making a significant difference. An alternative to a clothesline is a drying rack, which is available in many sizes and styles.

73 COMPUTE USING LESS ENERGY

With today's multi-computer households, lots of energy and hundreds of dollars can be saved by turning off your computer and monitor overnight. You save the power that's being used to run the computers, and in air-conditioned spaces you'll save on air-conditioning usage.

Other green computing strategies:

• **Enable the power management settings** on your computer. Doing so puts your computer, monitor, and hard drive in sleep mode after a period of inactivity you specify.

• **Buy an energy-efficient computer.** The average computer wastes half the electricity delivered to it. Check the Energy Star rating before you buy.

• **Buy a laptop.** Laptops use far fewer watts than desktops.

• **Plug your computer and peripherals into an outlet power strip.** It will make it easier to turn everything off when you're finished for the day.

For more ideas, check out climate-saverscomputing.org.

74 INSULATED PET DOORS

Pet doors are like big holes in the wall that allow wintry blasts to invade your home. Replace an old pet door with a new insulated unit. Double flaps create an air pocket that keeps heat in during the winter (and out in the summer). Look for (non-PVC) flaps with magnetic closures that are designed to stay flexible in very cold weather.

75 PUT ON A SWEATER

Brrrrr! It's a chilly February evening. So what do you do before crashing on the couch to watch a movie? Crank up the heat, of course. This is a quick-fix solution, sure, but it uses energy and costs money. Instead, try putting on an extra sweater, long underwear, and a pair of thick socks. Crawl under a blanket, too. These natural, energy-efficient methods can be just as effective as raising the thermostat or turning on the electric blanket. According to thedaily-green.com, an environmental Web site, putting on a light sweater will allow you to lower your thermostat by 2 degrees, which can save about 2 to 6 percent on your heating bill. You'll be comfortable on the most frigid February days…and you'll be warm on the inside, too, knowing you're doing your part.

Other ways to stay warm: drink hot chocolate or snuggle with a loved one.

76 CLEAN THE LINT TRAP

Taking the simple step of cleaning the lint trap (also known as the lint filter or lint screen) each time you use the dryer reduces a potential fire hazard. That's probably obvious. What may not be so obvious is that this act also saves energy. Hot air doesn't move through the dryer as efficiently when the lint trap is dirty, so the appliance has to work hotter and harder. Keeping the lint trap clean can decrease energy consumption by up to 30 percent. All that routine maintenance goes a long way to help extend the life of the dryer, too.

Don't toss that collection of fuzzy fabric particles into the trash, though. You can compost lint. It can also be used as mulch, as nesting material for birds, and as a fire-starter during your next camping trip.

77 STIR THE AIR

Ceiling fans are energy-efficient ways to stay cool in the summer. From a savings potential, however, they're even better at saving energy in the winter. That's because heat tends to rise and collect in the upper part of your rooms. Run your ceiling fan at a low speed and you'll circulate the warm air near the ceiling with the cooler air near the floor. Any energy used by the fan is more than offset by being able to lower the setting on your thermostat.

To prevent fires, keep electrical cords, drapery, and other furnishings at least 3 feet from the heater. Buy a unit with a tip-over safety switch.

78 USE SPACE HEATERS

Lower your thermostat and use space heaters to warm up only the rooms that are in use. Doing so is more efficient than heating the entire house—according to the Department of Energy, space heaters use about 14 percent of the energy that the average heating system does. When you'll only be in a room for a short period or you want to heat a small area, choose a radiant heater. (A radiant heater is typically filled with oil, but a more eco-friendly choice is one filled with water.) A convection heater circulates the air and is a better option when you want to heat an entire room. Portable heaters can be found in most home-improvement centers. Costs vary depending on what options (number of heat settings, oscillation, remote control, digital display, and so on) you desire. If you have children or pets, look for a heater that stays cool to the touch.

Everyone who lives where winters aren't too harsh should try warming up to the idea of turning down the heat in the house and using a space heater where the action is.

79 BURN CALORIES, NOT FUEL

If you've got a small job in the garden, in the garage, or in the house, use a hand tool that doesn't require electricity or gasoline. All that's required is a little muscle power. Eschew the power sprayer and use paintbrushes. Try a Yankee screwdriver instead of a cordless drill. Don't use a chain saw to remove those small limbs when lopping shears can do the job. Give up the electric log splitter and use a mechanical log splitter or a maul instead. Operate a manual can opener instead of an electric one. Put away the food processor to chop one onion and use a knife. These are just a few ways you can do a job greener. You've got the power, so don't always feel the need to power up a tool or appliance.

Using manual tools reduces noise pollution, too—other than some possible exertion grunts as you utilize your muscle power.

80 INSTALL HEAT TRAPS

Hot water tanks lose heat in several ways. The tank's built-in insulation, along with an aftermarket blanket or jacket, reduces loss from the tank but doesn't stop convective losses. These occur when hot water naturally circulates from the tank to the pipes that deliver water throughout the house. Heat traps, which are valves or loops of pipe and best added when installing a new hot water tank, will put a stop to convective losses. Some new tanks have factory-installed heat traps. Others offer them as options.

81 FILL THE FREEZER

A freezer consumes a lot of electricity. It doesn't use too much on a per-hour basis, but because it's on all the time, it puts a dent in the energy bill. You can save some electricity by keeping your freezer full. A freezer works most efficiently when it's full but not overloaded. The mass of the food holds temperatures better than the surrounding air. The freezer maintains its low temperature and thus doesn't have to run as often. You don't have to run out to the grocery store to buy items to fill the freezer. You can always fill plastic bottles or jugs with water. The water will help keep the freezer cold if the power goes out, and it comes in handy when you need ice for your next party.

82 GET WITH THE PROGRAM

When you're at work and the kids are at school—or when you're all away on vacation—it makes no sense to heat or cool an empty house. Installing a programmable thermostat, which automatically adjusts settings, will allow you to preset times when heating or air-conditioning units turn on. Program the thermostat to go off when you leave in the morning and come on about 30 minutes before you get home. Do the same thing when you sleep: keep it set low when you're in bed and program it to kick in when you wake up. You'll use less energy, without sacrificing comfort.

Programmable thermostats, which can store and repeat multiple daily settings, are easy to install and often cost less than $100—an amount you can save on your energy bill in the first year. According to the Department of Energy, you can save around 10 percent a year by lowering your thermostat 10 to 15 degrees for the duration of your 9-to-5 job.

Your thermostat's location can affect its performance. Keep it away from lighting, drafts, doorways, windows, appliances, and electronics. Interior walls are best.

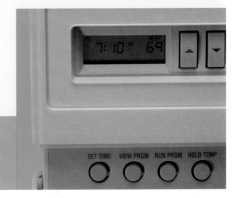

83 WATER HEATER BLANKETS

Water heaters account for up to 20 percent of the energy used in the average U.S. household. If your hot water heater is in an unheated space, such as an unfinished basement, insulate it and reduce your energy loss by 25 to 45 percent. Water heater blankets, or jackets, cost less than $30 and are easy to install. Spring for a slightly more expensive kit with a radiant barrier. It will insulate better than a fiberglass-only kit and is not prone to moisture damage. While you're at it, insulate the pipes that lead to and from your hot water heater, especially within 3 feet of the tank. Doing so will keep water in the pipes 2 to 4 degrees warmer, enabling you to lower your water temperature setting and save. As a bonus, the insulation will eliminate water condensation on pipes during humid weather. To save another 4 to 9 percent, place rigid insulation under your electric hot water tank—a job best done when installing a new unit.

84 SERVICE YOUR FURNACE

Hot air furnaces and boilers, whether oil or gas fired, should be serviced regularly by a professional. The serviceman will clean out ash accumulations that may be slowing heat transfer, optimize the burn, test electronic components, check belts for wear, and check for proper ventilation. This will not only add to the life of your equipment and improve safety but will ensure your system operates at its maximum efficiency.

85 OPEN THE CAR WINDOWS

Driving around town on a hot summer day? If you can do it, forgo the AC and instead roll down the windows and open the air vents to remain cool and comfortable. Your engine has to work harder to run an air-conditioning unit, which can increase emissions. Air conditioning can also lower your fuel economy by 10 to 20 percent, so it doesn't make much sense to use it when driving at slow speeds unless it's a truly scorching day. The best time to use the AC is when you're cruising down the highway, because open windows at high speeds create drag, which may result in worse mileage than you'd get using the air conditioner.

86 STOP DRAFTS COLD

In the winter, cold air can find its way into a home in many ways, including around windows and doors, through electrical outlet and switch openings, through attic and basement doors, and even through chimney flues. Add all the gaps together and it's equivalent to leaving a window wide open. Most infiltration can be stopped with weather stripping in one form or another. Each type is developed for a specific purpose.

For chimney flues, consider an inflatable chimney balloon or pillow. Insert it in the flue and inflate. The valve is designed to open and deflate the balloon should you forget it's there and start a fire.

Foam tape with adhesive backing is one of the easiest weather strippings to install. All you need is a pair of scissors.

87 REPLACE FURNACE FILTERS

One of the easiest and most important household chores is to change the filter on your forced hot-air heating system. A clogged filter resists airflow and makes your furnace work harder, lowering its efficiency and shortening its life. Expect to change your filter monthly or quarterly, depending on the type of filter you choose. You'll need to change it more often if you use your equipment for air conditioning in the summer, if you have pets, or if someone in your family has allergies.

Pleated filters last longer than disposable fiberglass panels and electrostatic panel filters. You can also reduce waste by using filters you can wash clean and reuse.

88 USE LED HOLIDAY LIGHTS

Clark Griswold sure was in the holiday spirit when he strung 25,000 incandescent lights on his house in *National Lampoon's Christmas Vacation*. Problem is, his display was consuming electricity faster than Rudolph pulls Santa's sleigh. To save energy and cut greenhouse gases, use LED (light-emitting diode) lights on trees and eaves and in holiday displays. LEDs are more expensive than traditional lights, but they consume less electricity—as much as 80 to 90 percent. They last much longer, too. A string of incandescent lights will last about 1,000 hours, but a string of LED lights can last 20 to 50 times longer. So you will likely save money in the long run.

Still not convinced LEDs are the way to go? Perhaps it will interest you to know that in 2007, for the first time ever, the Rockefeller Center Christmas Tree in New York City and the National Christmas Tree in Washington, D.C., were illuminated with energy-efficient LED lights.

If you're not yet ready to invest in a set of LEDs, put your conventional lights on a timer to decrease the amount of time they are on. And don't worry: even if you don't burn your lights all night long, Santa will find your house.

All will be merry and bright if you make the switch to LED holiday lights, which are actually tiny semiconductor chips, similar to computer chips.

89 SET YOUR PRIORITIES

It's late January. Your furnace is singing a high-pitched duet with the howling wind. You're wishing you had laid aside the golf clubs long enough to act on last summer's fleeting resolution to have your serviceman check out the rattle you heard last April. On top of that, the fuel company's latest bill just arrived, and it's a record breaker.

Time to buy a new furnace? Normally not. Most experts don't recommend replacement unless your furnace is at least 12 years old and in need of a costly repair, such as replacing a faulty heat exchanger or fried controller—or unless it's at least 16 years old, inefficient, and you live in a cold climate. (See "High-Efficiency Furnaces" on page 186.)

Even if your furnace's efficiency is not quite up to today's standards, it may make more sense to spend your money on low-cost, energy-saving improvements rather than $2,000 to $4,500 to install a new furnace. Putting in a setback thermostat, for example, can save up to 10 percent of your fuel bills.

90 KEEP THE ATTIC COOL

Attic spaces can reach temperatures of 160° F on a sunny summer day where outside temperatures are in the 90s. This will cause your air conditioner to work a lot harder to keep living space below the attic cool, especially if your attic has little or no insulation.

Reduce up to 30 percent of energy use for air conditioning by ensuring adequate attic ventilation. The optimal arrangement calls for vents in three places: along the roof's ridge, the soffits, and the gable ends. If you're unable to provide ventilation at all three places, consider a wind-assisted or thermostatically controlled power vent. The former, called a turbine vent, goes right on top of the roof. The latter is usually placed in the gable, and it can have louvers that automatically close to prevent dust or rain from entering when the fan is not in operation.

91 UNPLUG ELECTRONICS

Take a walk around the house and note how many items are plugged in. Some of the following likely make the list: lamps, TVs, DVD players, stereos, computers, printers, microwaves, blenders, toasters, coffeemakers, space heaters, fans, hair dryers, and chargers (for cell phones, cameras, iPods, and so forth).

Even when these items are turned off and in "standby" mode, they're using energy. According to the Department of Energy, 25 percent of the electricity used to power home electronics is consumed while the products are turned off. This is the reason your cell phone charger is warm when it's plugged in, even if the phone isn't connected. It's still drawing power. Don't sit idly by and allow your idle devices to waste this power. Get into the habit of unplugging appliances and electronics when not in use. Do so when you go to bed and before you leave for work, and definitely when you go on vacation.

92 RUN FULL LOADS

The average household washes hundreds of loads of dishes and clothes each year. If you run dishwashers and washing machines only when you have a full load, you won't do as many loads. This will save a lot of energy. Most of the energy used by a dishwasher goes to heat the water. You can't decrease the amount of water used per cycle, so maximize efficiency by filling your dishwasher. A washing machine requires about the same amount of energy to wash a pair of jeans and some socks that it does to wash a full load, so fill it up. If you have to do a small load, adjust the water level accordingly.

To save even more energy, consider using cold water—and cold-water-wash detergents— the next time you wash clothes.

93 USE OCCUPANCY SENSORS

With record electrical rates and one switch often controlling a half dozen fixtures, forgetting to turn off the lights can mean a huge waste of power and money. And who among us can claim that they (and their kids) are vigilant about turning off lights upon leaving a room? One solution is to install occupancy sensor-equipped light switches. For maximum savings, opt for a model that lets you turn on lights manually.

The lights remain on until the infrared (or ultrasonic sensor) no longer senses occupancy and turns them off. You can program a switch-off delay of 30 seconds to 30 minutes. Some switches also include a natural light sensor and will adjust lighting levels based on the room's natural light intensity, saving more electricity. Switches cost less than $50, install easily in existing switch boxes, and often return your investment in one to three years. Begin in rooms, where the lights are commonly left on.

CHAPTER 3

Reducing Waste

*T*he bad news: 33 billion paper checks were written last year. The good news: online bill payments now exceed paper payments among households with online access. Read on to find out more about this and other ways to wage war against waste.

C O N T E N T S

STOP JUNK MAIL

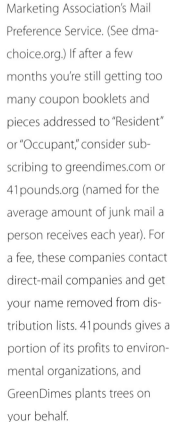

94

The typical American receives hundreds of pieces of junk mail each year, and millions of trees are cut down to bring these unwanted—and usually unopened—items to your mailbox. By putting an end to junk mail, you'll save trees and landfill space. You'll save time, too, because you won't have to sort through all those sweepstakes entries, catalogs, flyers, and so on. Opt out of most credit card and insurance offers by calling 888-567-8688. (It's free.) Stop most of the national advertising junk mail you receive by registering for free with the Direct Marketing Association's Mail Preference Service. (See dma-choice.org.) If after a few months you're still getting too many coupon booklets and pieces addressed to "Resident" or "Occupant," consider subscribing to greendimes.com or 41pounds.org (named for the average amount of junk mail a person receives each year). For a fee, these companies contact direct-mail companies and get your name removed from distribution lists. 41pounds gives a portion of its profits to environmental organizations, and GreenDimes plants trees on your behalf.

95 BUY LESS STUFF

We're a nation of consumers. The United States accounts for about 5 percent of the world's population but consumes more than 25 percent of the world's resources. According to the Environmental Protection Agency, each American creates about 4.5 pounds of garbage a day, which is twice what we made 35 years ago. Our consumer-driven lifestyles are filling up landfills at unprecedented rates. Here's a no-brainer way to ease this problem: buy less. Purchase only what you need. (Isn't 100 pairs of shoes a bit much? Isn't the new novel you want to read available at the library? Couldn't you borrow the tool you need from a neighbor?) Don't feel the need to upgrade (computers, cars, and the like) every year or two. If something is broken, fix it. Make a shopping list so you only get what you need. For the smarter consumer, less is truly more—more savings of resources, energy, and landfill space to be exact.

96 GO ELECTRONIC WITH FINANCIALS

The choice to go paperless can save billions of pounds of paper and thousands of trees every year in the United States. Begin by opting for direct deposit with your pay. Pay bills and receive bank statements electronically. If you invest in equities, have annual reports sent to you online. Another big paper savings: pay your taxes electronically.

97 COMMUNICATE ONLINE

Planning on putting pen to paper? Stop. Instead, put finger to keyboard. Communicating electronically saves trees and reduces waste. Everything from party invitations and church bulletins to birthday cards and PTA newsletters can be created on a computer and sent online.

In March 2007, the environmental Web site treehugger.com encouraged readers to add the following lines to their e-mail signatures in an effort to save paper: "Eco-Tip: Printing e-mails is usually a waste. Make this tip go viral, add it to your e-mail signature." We second the motion! The closer we can come to a paperless society, the better.

Stay in touch with friends by text-messaging or using social networking Web sites such as Facebook or MySpace.

"*The throwaway economy that has been evolving over the last half-century is an aberration, now itself headed for the junk heap of history.*"
— *Lester R. Brown*

98 SAVE AT THE OFFICE

Paper makes up about three-quarters of the waste in an office. According to the Environmental Protection Agency, each employee in a typical office generates 1.5 pounds of waste paper per day, and the average U.S. office worker uses 10,000 sheets of paper a year.

The solution? Use paper less, and use it more than once. Print only when it's a must. (Most documents, memos, invoices, and so forth can be viewed and sent on a computer.) Use double-sided printing, or flip over old printouts and use the blank side for faxes or scrap paper. If you must use copy paper, recycle it. If you keep a recycling bin near your desk you're more likely to recycle.

Recycle envelopes, cardboard boxes, batteries, toner and ink car-

A simple way to live greener at the office is to bring your own coffee mug and utensils. Use your mug at the water cooler, too

tridges, newspapers, magazines, bottles, and cans, too. Using refillable pens, pencils, and ink cartridges will also keep a lot of plastic and metal out of landfills.

99 NEW LIFE FOR OLD LINENS

Next time you clean out your closets, don't send those faded linens and tattered T-shirts to a landfill. Donate old sheets and towels to an animal shelter or a veterinarian's office. The towels can be used to dry off the animals, and the sheets provide some comfort as lining in a cage or kennel. Cut up old T-shirts and use them as rags. We learned of an eco-conscious individual who gets gratification from using her ex-boyfriend's old shirts to clean her toilet!

100 DISPOSE OF HHW RESPONSIBLY

The Environmental Protection Agency estimates that Americans generate 1.6 million tons of household hazardous waste (HHW) each year. What do you do with your HHW, which includes items such as paint, motor oil, batteries, and pesticides? Don't put them in the trash or dump them down the sink, toilet, or bathtub drain. The products may harm sanitation workers, and the volatile chemicals could contaminate the water supply. Some HHW is capable of igniting, exploding, corroding, or poisoning! See if your neighbor or a local business can use any of your excess HHW. Your community may have a permanent collection facility, it may hold collection days at a designated location, or it may have monthly or annual pickups. If you're not sure what hazardous-waste collection programs your town offers, ask! Contact your local environmental or solid-waste agency to find out how to get rid of your household hazardous waste, or visit earth911.org.

Not sure if what you have is hazardous? Read product labels for disposal instructions, or check online at epa.gov.

101 GIVE PEAS A CHANCE

You open the freezer door and you look…and look…and look. You're not really sure what's in there, or where anything is. Avoid those dreaded searches—with door ajar and energy bills climbing—by knowing what you have, and where you have it. This way, you won't waste energy—or food. If you can spot that pint of ice cream or that bag of peas, you're more likely to use these items before they go bad. It's an open-and-shut case.

Freezers often come without any shelving, which makes it a hassle to try to get something at the bottom of a pile. Add shelving to an existing unit or opt for drawers when buying new.

102 DON'T TOSS OLD ENVELOPES

Billions—yes, with a "B"—of envelopes are mailed each year. What's even better than recycling them? Reusing them. You can give new life to those preaddressed return envelopes by simply covering the address with a mailing label. Many of the envelopes you open can be reused, too, if you open them carefully. Some folks even turn envelopes they've opened inside out and reglue them to make new ones. If an envelope can't be used in the mail again, it could always live on as scrap paper or a storage device for coupons or seeds or school lunch money. And don't forget the envelopes you use at work. A lot of trees are cut down to make all those envelopes, and many of them end up in landfills. Reusing envelopes saves trees and reduces waste. Is reusing an envelope practical? Uh-huh. Frugal? Perhaps. Eco-friendly? You bet!

Want to make the most of an old envelope? Write your to-do list on one side, jot your grocery list on the other, and put anything you need—coupons, receipts, and so forth—inside. You're ready to go!

103 BIODEGRADABLE TRASH BAGS

Petroleum-based plastic trash bags live on for a l-o-n-g time in landfills. If you're willing to spend a little more money, you can use eco-friendly bags that will break down naturally in a matter of weeks or months, not decades or centuries. Companies such as BioBag (biobagusa.com) offer 100 percent biodegradable bags made from cornstarch (a renewable resource). In a controlled composting environment, BioBag products will decompose in 10 to 45 days; in a landfill, they'll break down at a rate comparable to paper, leaves, and other naturally biodegradable materials.

104 USE A DIGITAL CAMERA

The overwhelming majority of people use digital cameras, especially now that a nonprofessional photographer can get a quality camera—5 or 6 megapixels of resolution, some optical zoom, and a decent-sized LCD display—for less than $200.

If you're still shooting with a film camera, it's time to help the planet by going digital. Film is made with gelatin, a product extracted from the bones and connective tissues of cattle and other animals. Shooting digitally eliminates the use of animal products. Developing film is a chemically intensive process, and those chemicals—which often end up in landfills—can cause skin, eye, and lung irritation. Digital cameras render chemicals unnecessary. They save lots of paper, too. You can take a digital photo, view it (instantly!), save it, and share it with friends without having to print it. If you do print digital photos, you save paper by printing only the pictures you want. No need to develop an entire roll. If you still use a film camera, having your images burned on a CD instead of printed will save some paper.

Another nice thing about going digital: sharing photos by e-mail or on the Internet means you don't have to print them—and waste paper.

105 READ THE PAPER ONLINE

Sitting at the table with your morning coffee and newspaper in hand, perusing the headlines, and tackling the crossword may be a tough habit to break, but it's one worth considering. Acres and acres of trees are used to make the more than 50 million newspapers that are printed each day. If everybody switched to reading the paper online, we'd save approximately 500,000 trees each week. Cancel your home-delivery subscription and subscribe for online delivery instead. We doubt you'll miss that pile of newspapers in your kitchen or the ink on your fingertips.

Even better, an online paper is often free. (*The New York Times* became free in 2007.) Some papers, such as *The Wall Street Journal,* have a fee to access all content, but it's still usually less expensive than a print subscription. Many Web pages can be customized so you immediately get the news you want the most, whether it's the latest football scores or the weather forecast or the day's top headlines. Go on a paper diet. Check out onlinenewspapers.com, which has links to thousands of papers from all over the world. Some of them offer the printed version online in PDF form. If you must have the real thing, recycle it!

106 USE THE LIBRARY

It doesn't take a Hogwarts education to know that 20 people reading the same copy of a Harry Potter book is much less wasteful than 20 people each buying their own copy of the same book. Besides, how many books do you own that you've read once and will never look at again? They sit on your shelves, collecting dust. Hopping on your Nimbus 2000 broom and heading to your local library—there are more than 16,000 public libraries in the United States—is a great way to conserve resources and reduce waste. Check out a book or DVD. Listen to a CD. Read today's newspaper. It won't cost you a penny. Libraries are wonderful resources, and most of them have all the latest bestsellers, so if you're looking for Harry Potter, you'll find him.

For those of you who are dedicated to leaving the smallest footprint possible, many libraries offer computers for public use.

107 MAKE IT LAST LONGER

Through careful maintenance, you can get years of additional service from almost everything you own, including tools, clothing, and electronics. The longer you can make things last, the more resources and energy you save. The exception is if you own extremely wasteful things, such as a gas-guzzling SUV or a 30-year-old furnace. Replacing inefficient cars and appliances will often save energy in the long run. Your best ally in maintaining things is the owner's manual that came with the equipment. Keep it filed in a safe place, along with lists of authorized repair shops.

Cleanliness is one of the keys to long tool life.

108 GO DIAPER FREE

Potty-train your baby right from day one by learning "elimination communication." Once you know what to look for, you can read your baby's body language and anticipate when he is going to go to the bathroom. You hold him over the toilet and give the "go ahead" signal, which the baby soon learns to wait for. The result? You save an estimated 8,000 disposable diapers from the landfill and avoid exposing your baby to questionable chemicals in plastic diapers. While a bit radical for the average American, this technique has been used for thousands of years and is still used today in some cultures. If going diaper free isn't for you, new cloth diapers with a flushable inner liner are a good choice—they avoid a lot of the washing that makes traditional cloth diapers a drain on the environment.

109 REKINDLE AN OLD FLAME

Break the habit of using disposable lighters and return to good old matches. They don't use up nearly as many petroleum resources, either for fuel or manufacture, and are biodegradable. If you choose wooden matches, opt for those from companies that harvest from well-managed forests. If you can't live without a lighter, choose a refillable model. It may seem like a small act of kindness to the planet, but more than 1 billion disposable lighters are sold annually in the United States alone.

110 USE REFILLABLE PENS

According to Green Seal, Americans discard 1.6 million pens every year. Placed end to end, they would stretch more than 150 miles. Some of these disposable pens—which are often made from dangerous PVC—get recycled. Many of them end up in the dump. Reduce waste by using refillable pens and pencils. The casing is used again and again. All you have to purchase are the refills (or, better yet, ink), which are less expensive than new pens and pencils. For an assortment of environmentally friendly refill supplies, check out greenearthofficesupply.com. If you want to do the "write" thing for the earth, start using refillable pens and pencils.

111 USE SCRAP PAPER

An easy way to save trees is to reuse waste paper as scrap paper. The blank side of documents, photocopies, faxes, envelopes, and page-a-day calendar pages can be given new life. Letter-size paper can be used for photocopies, printouts, or faxes. Smaller pieces are perfect for making grocery lists or to-do lists, taking phone messages, leaving instructions for the baby-sitter, or sticking a love note in your spouse's lunch. Scrap paper can also be used as a bookmark or in art projects. Reuse instead of buying new.

112 BYOB

No, not Bring Your Own Beer. Try Bring Your Own Bag. To the store, that is. Grocery bags pile up quickly—if they make it home. Many of the more than 380 million plastic bags used in the United States each year float away with the breeze, becoming litter. As they break down (very slowly), they pollute our soil and water. They sometimes find their way to a bird or marine mammal, which mistakes them for food, chokes, and dies. To keep this clutter out of your home—and to keep nonbiodegradable plastic bags out of landfills—bring your own bag to the supermarket. Use a sturdy canvas or cloth bag that is roomy enough to hold what you plan to purchase. Chances are, you have one or two of these reusable bags lying in the back of a closet. (If not, many supermarkets now sell them.) Keep a bag or two in the car, ready to use at all times. Or put your reusable bags near the door so you can take them on your way out.

According to reusablebags.com, an estimated 500 billion to 1 trillion plastic bags are consumed worldwide each year. Save the petroleum and use a reusable bag.

113 BUY FAMILY SIZE

It almost always makes sense to purchase larger sizes. In addition to saving significant amounts of money, you'll reduce the number of shopping trips you make—saving time, gasoline, and more money. There's also a good chance you'll reduce the amount of wasteful packaging that comes with your purchases. Take toothpaste, for example. One large tube holds more than seven or eight small ones, costs less per ounce, and uses less plastic in its manufacture. Ditto for almost anything you can think of, including water, tissues, shampoo, shaving cream, mouthwash, and dishwashing and laundry detergents. If you don't like having to use big containers at home, many items—especially liquids—can be easily poured into smaller dispensers. Buying in bulk saves more money and reduces packing waste, too. A large bag of napkins uses a lot less plastic packing than a bunch of small packages.

114 WRAP GIFTS GREENLY

Don't get "wrapped up" in the need to buy wrapping paper. It creates waste and fills landfills to the tune of millions of tons per year. Instead, use what you've got around the house. Use the sports section of the newspaper for the gift for the sports enthusiast or the funnies for a child. Wrapping in fabric, which is reusable, is also a better option than paper, which is usually used once and thrown away. If you do use wrapping paper, buy recycled versions, not the stuff made from virgin paper. And do without the ribbons, bows, and boxes; gifts can be accented with pine cones or handmade ornaments instead. The best thing for the planet, of course, is to forgo all wrapping, though this might not go over well with some young children. Instead, try placing gifts in decorative tins or hiding them as part of a "gift hunt." If you receive a wrapped gift, unwrap it carefully so the paper can be used again.

115 BRING YOUR OWN CUP

Walk by the trash at your favorite coffee shop. Chances are good you'll see plenty of paper, plastic, or—gasp!—foam cups. What a waste. According to the green Web site Ideal Bite (idealbite.com), if you buy a cup of coffee in a disposable container each day, you create about 23 pounds of waste per year. Say no to disposable cups—and, for that matter, utensils—and carry your own container. Keep a mug at the office for those afternoon caffeine fixes. Keep a travel mug or tumbler in the car, and use it to fill up on java at the gas station or coffee shop. Some coffee shops, such as Sip Café in Nashville, Tennessee, offer discounts to people who bring in their own reusable containers. Starbucks takes 10 cents off for customers who bring their own mugs. (In 2004, Starbucks customers used their own mugs 15.1 million times, keeping 655,000 pounds of paper waste out of landfills.) Western Washington University's "Recycle Mug" program encourages customers to reduce their use of disposable cups by offering an incentive—a $1.19 refill price for coffee and soda is offered to all customers who present a reusable mug.

116 USE PAPERLESS BILLING

Each month, the phone bill arrives in the mail. The bill, which seemingly has more pages than a small novel, comes with a return envelope and advertising inserts for items you'll never buy. Each month, you write out a check for said phone bill. Bills, envelopes, inserts, checks—what a waste of paper. Using paperless billing, if that option is available, saves trees. (In 2006, Verizon Wireless processed more than 70 million online payments, reducing paper usage by more than 400 tons.) It saves trips to the post office and money spent on stamps, too. With just a click of a mouse you can access your account, view your bill, and make a secure payment. Some companies even allow you to schedule regular payments for recurring bills—everything from car loans to mortgage payments. Funds are automatically transferred from your checking or savings account, or from a credit or debit card.

117 SEND E-CARDS

Aghast at the cost of greeting cards? Stop contributing to the tons of paper waste, pollution from inks, and the energy lost to delivering traditional cards. Send your cards online instead. Web sites such as americangreetings.com, 123greetings.com, and e-cards.com allow you to send animated e-cards and cards with your personal digital photos to anyone with an e-mail address. Select from dozens of card categories, including holiday, get-well, and anniversary. Some e-cards are free. For most, however, you'll have to pay for a subscription that's about equal to buying a few traditional greeting cards.

118 MAKE YOUR OWN COMPOST

Although a rich, deep brown when fully "cooked," compost is "green" in several ways. It improves the vitality of flowers and vegetable plants, keeps moisture from draining or evaporating too quickly from the soil, and makes use of organic materials that would otherwise have simply added to overburdened landfills and incinerators. To be successful at making your own compost, you'll need to nourish the billions of microbes that do the work with the right balance of moisture, air, and food. The moisture content of a compost pile or bin should be about 50 percent, or about as moist as a sponge that has been wrung. To aerate, turn the pile and break up clumps with a garden fork. Use yard and kitchen wastes to feed the hardworking microbes. Add equals amount of "green" waste (weeds, clippings, green leaves, fruit, animal manures, and vegetable scraps) and "brown" waste (dry weeds, straw, wood chips, brown leaves, and newspaper). Don't compost human or pet feces, meat, bones, diseased plants, or wood that has been treated with preservatives.

Countertop compost pails and biodegradable bags make composting easier and less messy.

119 BED DOWN ON BAMBOO

When it comes to bed sheets, comfort is a must. Turns out, you can be comfy under sheets made of 100 percent bamboo fiber. What's nice about that is bamboo is a sustainable resource that can be harvested every three to six years. It's grown with little or no pesticides, and it requires very little water.

Bamboo sheets, which are available in all sizes, are soft, breathable, and anti-bacterial. They've got a silky feel, too. Bamboo isn't a completely green choice because it's an imported product and because the process of turning the stalk into fiber may not always be handled in the most eco-friendly manner, but it still makes less of an impact on the environment than cotton, which is grown with lots of pesticides, lots of water, and petroleum-based synthetics. You can rest easy when you decide to bed down with bamboo.

120 MAKE SPONGES LAST LONGER

Most people use a sponge for only a couple of weeks before tossing it. If regularly—and properly—cared for, however, those weeks can turn to months. Wring sponges after each use. Every three to five days, disinfect sponges, which are probably the most contaminated item in your house because they provide a warm, moist environment for bacteria to grow. To disinfect, boil sponges in a pot of water for five minutes or microwave them for two minutes. Be sure they are wet because the sponges must be *boiled*. Allow them to dry completely between uses. Rotate a couple of sponges, so you have one ready to use while the other is being disinfected. Don't run sponges through the dishwasher. Studies have shown that this method doesn't get them entirely clean. Nor does soaking them in lemon juice or a bleach solution.

Make petroleum-based sponges last longer by regularly wringing, rotating, and disinfecting them. Boiling is the surest way to do the latter.

121 DOWNLOAD YOUR MUSIC

A lot goes into that "The Joshua Tree" U2 CD you own. Think about the waste and pollution created to process, manufacture, ship, and ultimately, discard the CD, complete with jewel case, liner notes, and shrink wrap. You can help the environment by purchasing songs (along with movies, TV shows, and audiobooks) online. Consider: Apple CEO Steve Jobs announced at Macworld Expo 2008 that his company's iTunes Store sold 20 million songs on Christmas Day in 2007. If you estimate a dozen songs on an average CD, that's the equivalent of 1.67 million CDs, which is quite a bit to keep out of the trash in one day.

Download your music. Bono would be proud.

Songs of musicians from A (AC/DC) to Z (ZZ Top) are available for downloading, so forgo the CDs and put your favorite tunes onto computers and digital audio players.

122 ECO-FRIENDLY PACKAGING

When you ship something, don't use petroleum-based bubble wrap or, even worse, foam peanuts. Both materials end up in landfills after they're discarded. Bubble wrap takes hundreds of years to break down, and the foam peanuts never completely break down. Fortunately, you have a few earth-friendly options. Instead of throwing away old sheets of paper, shred them and use them as packing material. Crumple the daily newspaper and give it new life as packing material before it reaches the recycle bin. Some people even use bags of leaves as cushioning—the leaves can be composted after the package arrives. And don't overlook biodegradable packing peanuts made out of cornstarch, which are available at most office-supply stores. If you're moving, don't waste money on bubble wrap and foam peanuts. Use old newspapers, clothes, towels, and bed sheets to cushion your belongings.

123 AVOID EXCESS PACKAGING

A good portion of the money you spend at the supermarket goes toward packaging. A good portion of that packaging ends up in landfills. To reduce waste, avoid items with excess packaging. If possible, purchase goods with no packaging. For example, don't buy pre-washed lettuce in a bag when you can get a head of lettuce instead. According to a 2007 report on packaging efficiency by the editors of The ULS Report (ULS stands for Use Less Stuff), the best way to reduce waste is through the use of flexible packaging—bags and pouches instead of rigid containers. Try coffee in a bag instead of a can. Look for tuna in a pouch instead of a can. The study also noted that single-serve items result in increased waste, so stay away from the box of single-serve chip bags and buy one big bag. And when you are looking for a cool drink to quench your thirst, purchase large beverage bottles instead of individual cans and juice boxes.

124 REDUCE WATER BOTTLE WASTE

Americans have a love affair with drinking bottled water, though it's not an earth-friendly habit. Lots of energy is consumed processing, manufacturing, and transporting the petroleum-based plastic bottles. And most of those bottles end up in landfills. But bottled water is better for me, you say. Not true. It offers no relative health benefits. In fact, bottled water is less regulated than tap water and undergoes less testing. The Food and Drug Administration regulates the former as a packaged food product, and the Environmental Protection Agency regulates the latter. But bottled water tastes better, you say. Not true. In many taste tests, subjects prefer tap water. If you're not one of those people, you can always use a filter. Bottled water is more expensive, you say. That's for sure. Many people have no problem forking over a buck for a 20-ounce bottle. At that price, bottled water is $6.40 per gallon—about two times the average price of gas! Drinking bottled water is not healthier for you, and it's definitely not healthier for the planet. Try the tap.

If you want your water on the go, use a long-lasting, nontoxic water bottle.

CHAPTER 4

Growing Green

Growing plants contributes to the ecosystem by filtering CO_2 and emissions from the air, producing oxygen, maintaining wildlife, and helping to conserve soil and water. That we can often eat as well as admire what we grow is a healthy bonus.

CONTENTS

GROW AN ORGANIC LAWN

125

With a little extra care, you can eliminate petrochemicals from your lawn-maintenance routine. Begin by testing your soil to find out what to add to get the soil's pH right and to replace depleted nutrients. Try using only slow-release natural fertilizers, such as composted manure, bone meal, and dried poultry waste. Reduce the chance for disease and insect infestation—along with the need for herbicides and pesticides—by not cutting grass too short, avoiding overfertilization, always using a sharp mower blade, dethatching and aerating, top-dressing with compost, and watering deeply but less frequently. When planting a new lawn, choose a low-maintenance cultivar that's tailored for your region. (See page 95.) Check out products such as corn gluten meal, a nontoxic preemergent herbicide that can keep crabgrass and many other weeds from developing roots.

An organic lawn may not look as perfect as a chemically enhanced lawn, but it will be healthier for people, pets, and wildlife.

126 CONVERT TO IPM YARD CARE

For many years, insects have been viewed as invaders that should be attacked with toxic chemicals. While such actions may take care of the immediate problem, they usually create a host of others. Integrated Pest Management, or IPM, is a better choice. With IPM, the yard is viewed as an ecosystem with components that are interdependent and where every action has a wide-ranging impact. The goal of IPM is to keep insects, as well as diseases and weeds, at tolerable levels using the least toxic methods available. Techniques include planting pest-resistant cultivars, following appropriate lawn-care practices, inspecting regularly for problems, encouraging beneficial insects, and spot-treating affected areas. Let's face it: bugs are here to stay. Most of them are actually desirable and serve a purpose, such as decomposition. Others are considered beneficial because their diet includes the insects chomping on your grass. Studies have shown that predators such as ants and ground beetles are able to remove up to 74 percent of Japanese beetle eggs and up to 53 percent of fall armyworm pupae from pesticide-free plots within 48 hours. Before reaching for the insecticide, wait a while to give these natural enemies of pests a chance to bring your problem under control.

127 BUILD A GREENHOUSE

A greenhouse is a great way to capture free energy and turn it into vegetables, flowers, or ornamental plants. All you need is a sunny spot that's sheltered from strong winds. Kits are available in a wide variety of sizes and price ranges. Long-lasting units are made with extruded aluminum and glazed with glass or acrylic. Cheaper units are all plastic, but they don't last as long. The least expensive option is to build your own using lumber and heavy-mil polyethylene sheeting for glazing.

Greenhouses are great for starting plants earlier in the spring and extending your growing season in the fall. If you live in a cold climate, where the thermometer dips below freezing regularly, winter use of your greenhouse may be cost prohibitive because it would require the use of a gas heater at night.

"*Until you dig a hole, you plant a tree, you water it and make it survive, you haven't done a thing. You are just talking.*"
— Wangari Maathai

This prefabricated, extruded aluminum unit is available in many sizes and with several glazing options. Solar-powered vent openers keep the inside from overheating on sunny days.

Favorite houseplants range from low-care cactuses to rare tropical specimens, but to be really eco-correct, choose plants that are native to your area—or that have been propagated nearby.

128 GROW MORE INDOORS

Houseplants, such as English ivy, spider plant, and rubber plants, will help detoxify the air in your home by absorbing traces of formaldehyde, benzene, carbon monoxide, and other nasty gases. They also add oxygen and help maintain balanced humidity. But you'll need to grow more than an African violet or two to get the job done. Experts recommend one good-size plant for every 100 square feet of living space.

129 BE A HERITAGE GARDENER

Buy heirloom seeds and preserve the genetic diversity of our seed resources for future generations. Heirloom seeds are nonhybrid and usually organic, unlike many of today's varieties that have been engineered and genetically modified for the convenience of commercial growers.

Black tomatoes, bull nose peppers, and Healy's melons are just a few of the heirloom varieties available.

130 BUY ORGANIC SEED

If you're planting an organic garden, it makes sense to buy and support organic seed producers. In doing so, you will ensure that your seeds were grown using sustainable methods and that they are free of genes or traits from an unrelated species. Organic seeds should have USDA Organic certification. Check the supplier's Web site for its certification number, certifying agent, and date of last annual inspection.

131 PLANT A RAIN GARDEN

Storm water runoff from compacted lawns, roofs, and driveways is one of the largest sources of water pollution across the United States because chemicals, such as lawn fertilizers, pesticides, and automotive fluids, are flushed into storm drains and natural bodies of water. Surges of storm water, even when not laden with chemicals, can overload sewers, cause flooding, and destroy wildlife habitats.

You can capture runoff before it enters sewers and natural water sources with a rain garden. Planted in natural depressions, rain gardens typically comprise native plants that don't mind occasional "wet feet." They can include ferns, rushes, wildflowers, shrubs, and small trees. Once established they require less maintenance than lawns because they do not need mowing, fertilizer, or watering.

By slowing storm water runoff, rain gardens promote better water quality through filtration and help recharge natural aquifers.

132 IMPROVE YOUR YARD SOIL

Soil is one of the main pillars of life on earth. If you're fortunate enough to own a patch of it, treat it kindly. Obviously, you should never dump or spill anything that might be harmful, such as motor oil, pesticides, or herbicides, but there are other things you can do to enhance it should you want to grow things. First, test it for pH balance and nutrients. University labs, through the auspices of your area's cooperative extension service, will tell you what your soil needs. Aerate areas that have been compacted by traffic or vehicles. Address situations where erosion is a problem by regrading or digging in subsurface trenches, swales, berms, or terraces.

In a lawn, yellowish grass and the presence of plantains and crabgrass are signs of poor soil.

Most herbs prefer soil that is well drained and need at least six hours of full sun to develop the oil content that ensures good flavor.

133 GROW HERBS FOR HEALTH

Fresh herbs are often sold in wasteful plastic packaging for astronomical prices. Common sage can cost $20 per pound! You can supply all your needs for the entire year in a 4 x 8-foot plot. Best of all, herbs are easy to grow. They don't require rich soil—just plenty of sun and occasional watering.

Preserving herbs is simple, too. To freeze them, lay them flat on a tray. Then put them in an airtight container and leave them frozen until needed. To dry herbs, hang the branches upside down in a brown paper bag with holes in it.

134 PLANT A WINDBREAK

By strategically planting evergreen trees, hedges, and shrubs to create a windbreak for your house, you can save as much as 20 percent of your winter heating bills. A windbreak that is tall and full enough can also serve as a privacy screen. Choose a spot about 50 feet from the house, facing the direction of the prevailing wind in winter. It should be 50 feet wider than the house on both ends. When choosing your trees, select species that will grow tall enough to make a difference. A windbreak is effective for a distance of about 30 times its height. For example, a windbreak that's 20 feet tall will reduce winds for a distance of about 600 feet. The area you wish to protect, such as a house or patio, should fall within this protected zone.

If space is tight, you can plant a small windbreak so it ends up being 4 or 5 feet from the house once the shrubs mature. It will shield the house from the wind, and the dead air space between the house and the windbreak will help serve as an insulator.

135 DOWNSIZE YOUR LAWN

The American lawn is based on the big-lawn tradition of English aristocracy. In the long run, it's as unsustainable as kings and queens. Begin now to reduce the square footage of your lawn to what you actually need for backyard recreation and entertainment. Turn the rest over to native plantings, fruit trees, and vegetable gardens. If you can make the lawn small enough, you'll be able to opt for a nonpolluting manual or electric mower. In addition, a smaller lawn will be easier to grow organically, without toxic herbicides, pesticides, and petroleum-based fertilizers. It will also cut down on water usage.

A heavy layer of mulch and ground covers, such as hosta, can help reduce lawn size and pollution.

136 ENCOURAGE BENEFICIALS

Helpful bugs will assist you in keeping the bad guys out of your garden and off your lawn—and they're a lot more eco-friendly than pesticides that kill off good and bad alike. Lady beetles and lacewings, for example, have an appetite for aphids. Ground beetles have a taste for beetle grubs, caterpillars, army-worms, and cutworms. Big-eyed bugs go after chinch bugs and others. Attract beneficial insects with flowering plants that are rich in nectar and pollen, including bee balm, purple coneflower, Queen Anne's lace, and thyme.

137 PRESERVE A TREE

A mature tree can provide all sorts of benefits, from saving energy to provid-ing wildlife habitat. (See "Plant a Tree in Your Yard" on page 99.) Neglect or improper maintenance, however, can kill a mature tree in a few seasons. Keep your trees healthy by:

• **Practicing correct pruning.** Hire only trained landscaping professionals.

• **Not cutting or damaging roots,** most of which live near the soil surface.

• **Not burying roots** with soil when regrading, which can smother the tree.

• **Leaving a branch collar** when pruning branches. The branch collar has cells and chemicals that block decay and diseases.

Surveys have shown that a wooded property where the trees have been properly maintained is worth up to 15 percent more than a barren lot.

138 DETER WEEDS NATURALLY

When looking at large areas of lawn contaminated by weeds, most people resort to herbicides. Unfortunately, many herbicides pose health risks for you and every living thing that comes in contact with them. Corn gluten meal, a powdery byproduct from the manufacture of corn starch and corn syrup, is a nontoxic alternative. Spread it on your lawn to control many types of broadleaf weeds, including crabgrass, dandelion, and purslane. Corn gluten meal is a preemergent herbicide that works by inhibiting root formation. The time of the application is critical. Ideally, it should be applied three to five weeks before the target weeds are due to germinate, typically in mid-to-late spring.

Corn gluten meal, which is 10 percent nitrogen, also serves as a slow-release fertilizer. It is available at most nurseries and home centers, and it sells under dozens of brand names.

139 SELECT AN ECO-FRIENDLY SEED

If you're planting a new lawn, you have the rare opportunity of selecting the latest and most eco-friendly seed recommended for your region. Today's cultivars (seeds that have been cultivated to exhibit appealing characteristics) require less water, fertilizer, and pesticides. Some are slower growing, thereby reducing the number of times you must mow. Contact your local Cooperative Extension Service for the recommended cultivar in your region. Other excellent resources are the National Turfgrass Evaluation Program (NTEP) and the Guelph Turfgrass Institute in Ontario, Canada.

140 MAKE THE SWITCH

Choose an organic lawn care company over one that uses petroleum-derived fertilizers, pesticides, and herbicides. Organic lawn care companies are sprouting up around the country. Their programs use only natural products made from vegetable protein meals. Organic lawn care services promise a healthy, green lawn that's relatively weed free after one to three years of treatment, depending on how weed infested your lawn is at the start.

Organic lawn care will not eliminate every weed, so some attitude adjustment—and some hand-weeding—may be necessary.

141 BE BEE FRIENDLY

Bees pollinate food crops and make our gardens blossom, but bee populations worldwide are shrinking because of disease and development. You can help boost local bee populations in several ways:

• **Plant flowers.** They provide pollen and nectar sources vital to the survival of bees. Choose native flowers that bloom successively over the spring, summer, and fall, and arrange them in clusters that are colorful and contrast well with their environment. Purple and blue are bees' favorite colors, followed by yellow and orange.

• **Provide a source of water,** such as a pond or birdbath.

• **Avoid the use of pesticides.** If you must, choose the least-toxic product and apply in the late evening when most bees have gone into the hive for the evening.

• **Leave piles** of undisturbed leaves or brush where possible to create a natural place for wild bees to nest.

• **Don't touch weeds** that bees are attracted to, such as white clover and dandelions.

4

GROWING GREEN

Bees and other pollinators are attracted to purplish hues, so lavender (shown) and wisteria are favorites.

365 WAYS TO LOVE THE PLANET **97**

142 PLANT A CUTTING GARDEN

Commercially grown flowers rely heavily upon fertilizers and pesticides derived from petrochemicals. In addition, energy is expended with the shipping and refrigeration of plants as they are readied for sale. Throw in your own drive to the flower shop, and you can begin to understand why planting your own cutting garden is a greener way to put a bouquet on the dining-room table—a cutting garden will also beautify your yard. If you don't have time for gardening, take a careful look around. Roadside fields—and even vacant lots—are loaded with material for beautiful floral arrangements, free for the picking.

Plant an extra plot of flowers expressly for cutting. Choose varieties that won't quickly wilt in a vase.

143 DECK THE WALLS WITH VINES

Save cooling costs in the summer by installing a trellis on your south-facing exterior wall and growing deciduous vines on it. Jasmine, grape, and ivy are popular choices. The vines will absorb and reflect the sun's energy in the summer. In the winter, the energy will reach the wall or window and warm the surface. Do not plant vines directly on the wall or you may damage the siding, even if it is brick or stone. Make trellises removable so you can get to the wall to maintain it. Vines will also help to reduce noise and dust pollution.

144 PLANT A TREE IN YOUR YARD

In addition to the natural beauty of trees, they can also reduce your energy bill. Plant deciduous trees about 20 feet to the southeast and southwest of your home, and they will provide cooling shade through much of the morning and late afternoon in the summer. When the leaves drop, they will allow the warming rays of the sun to pass through. Choose trees that will grow at least 10 feet higher than the window you hope to shade.

Trees also do a lot for the environment—preventing erosion, filtering dust and pollutants from the air, lessening noise, and creating habitats for animals and birds. Choose tree species that are native to your area for the best results.

Walnut trees can be grown in much of the United States. Choose a Butternut (white) Walnut variety (shown) over a Black Walnut for best eating.

145 GROW YOUR OWN NUTS

Take more tractor-trailer trucks off the road by collecting your own nuts. A great source of protein, grafted cultivars will bear fruit in two or three years. Trees grown on their own roots will bear fruit in six or more years. Common nut varieties that can be grown in many zones in the United States include almond, hazelnut, pecan, and walnut. Check with your local county extension agents about varieties suited to your region. No space or time to grow your own? Locate nut-bearing trees in your locale. Many are on public property and free for the picking once they fall to the ground.

When raspberries stop producing, wineberries (above) are just beginning. Soon after, it will be time to harvest blackberries.

146 PICK YOUR OWN BERRIES

Commercially grown berries must be carefully harvested and packaged to prevent bruising and then quickly shipped to market to prevent them from going bad. That makes them an energy-intensive food—unless of course you grow your own. All you need is a sunny area in your yard.

Choose cultivars that bear at different times of the year so you'll have many months of picking. You can also choose early and late varieties. Strawberries, for example, can be both spring and fall bearing.

Many berries grow wild and are yours for the picking—if you can beat the birds to them! Look for them along the edges of wooded areas.

147 JOIN A COMMUNITY GARDEN

Whether you live in a place where you cannot have your own garden or simply enjoy gardening with others, joining a community garden may be for you. A community garden is any plot of land where individuals grow flowers, fruits, or vegetables.

Check out the American Community Gardening Association Web site (communitygarden.org) for a city or zip code listing of community gardens. If it doesn't list one near you, inquire with your local cooperative extension agent. In addition to food production, community gardens can preserve green space in urban areas, reduce crime, reduce city heat, and encourage social interaction.

148 DISCOVER GROUND COVERS

Ground covers offer an eco-friendly alternative to lawns. They use less fertilizer and water, don't need to be mowed, and are often vigorous enough to crowd out weeds. Use them in low-traffic areas or in areas where grass doesn't thrive, such as in shady places or on slopes subject to erosion. Make your plant selections carefully. Shade-loving ground covers include bishop's hat, English ivy, European wild ginger, lily-of-the-valley, hosta, and sweet woodruff. For partial shade to sun, opt for bugleweed, lilyturf, daylily, pachysandra, mondo grass, periwinkle (myrtle), or St. John's wort. In full sun, cotoneaster, juniper, and many types of ornamental grasses thrive.

149 GROW YOUR VEGETABLES

It makes less and less sense to ship produce thousands of miles to supermarkets when you can grow most of what you need a few yards from your back door. All that's required is a sunny exposure, about 50 square feet per family member, access to running water, a few simple tools, and a good back. In addition to eliminating all the energy use that goes into shipping and packaging, you'll be able to choose tastier varieties and grow them organically, without chemical fertilizers and pesticides.

Vegetable gardening is a rewarding pastime, but don't fool yourself. Without at least six hours of full sun (preferably more) you will not be successful.

"The very spot where grew the bread that formed my bones, I see. How strange, old field, on thee to tread, and feel I'm part of thee."
— Abraham Lincoln

150 BEFRIEND BUTTERFLIES

Most of the suggestions in this book are about practical matters: reducing waste and pollution, conserving water and energy, and so forth. In this entry, however, our pitch is to preserve beauty—and few would disagree that butterflies (and many moths) are among nature's most beautiful creatures. Unfortunately, like songbirds, amphibians, and many other species, butterfly populations are under stress due to habitat destruction. Give butterflies a boost in your yard by planting a butterfly-friendly garden. Include nectar-producing flowers that nourish adults, such as butterfly bush and butterfly weed. Also include food plants required by butterfly larva. Each species has its own preferences. Black swallowtail caterpillars, for example, like dill, parsley, fennel, and carrot plants. Monarch caterpillars prefer milkweed.

Need a practical reason to nurture butterflies? They also help pollinate both wild plants and crops.

151 OPT FOR NATIVE PLANTS

When shopping at your local nursery for trees and shrubs, opt for plants that are native to your region. If you're unsure

about what's native, contact your local cooperative extension agent. Avoid invasive plants—those that are alien to your local ecosystem. Invasive plants have devastated the landscape in many areas of the United States. They have also changed habitats to the point where they have contributed to the decline of endangered species—both plants and animals.

Cultivating native plants in your yard will reduce your reliance on irrigation, fertilizer, and pesticides.

152 BUILD A LIVING FENCE

It takes thousands of board feet to build a fence—even more wood than it takes to build the wall of a room! It also requires gallons of paint or stain every few years to keep it looking good. Rather than waste such a valuable resource, try growing your next fence. It takes only posts, rails, and vigorous vines to accomplish what would otherwise require dozens of boards. In place of pickets, choose from clematis, roses, wisteria, grape, or any of dozens of other flowering vines.

A growing fence is more pleasing to look at than a traditional fence. It costs less to build, too.

153 PLANT AN ORCHARD

Take a cue from Johnny Appleseed and plant your own fruit trees. You'll no longer have to deal with supermarket produce that looks good but never seems to ripen or taste the way you believe fruits should. Generally, fruit trees should be planted 15 to 20 feet apart to avoid crowding at maturity. Choose a sunny location with well-drained soil. Consider placing beehives in your orchard to help with pollination.

Newly developed rootstocks (plants with established roots upon which the desired cultivar is grafted) allow you to grow dwarfed trees in small spaces, harvest fruit in as little as two or three years, and prune and pick without the need for climbing a ladder.

Flat-trained fruit trees, shaped in cordons, espaliers, and fans, take up even less space. They can be grown against walls, trellises, or fences. Choose from apples, apricots, cherries, nectarines, figs, peaches, pears, and plums.

CHAPTER 5

Reuse & Recycle

*T*he first rule of waste management is to reuse the product or material you no longer need. The second is to recycle it, either for its original purpose or a new one. Either way, doing so will divert material from landfills, and save energy and resources.

CONTENTS

GIVE FREECYCLE A SPIN

154

You've heard the adage "one man's trash is another man's treasure." The Freecycle Network (freecycle.org), a nonprofit organization that began in 2003 and now has more than 4,000 groups and 4 million members around the world, knows this is true.

That's why the grassroots movement promotes the free exchange of second-hand or unwanted goods—everything from school supplies and stuffed animals to paintings and pianos—in your area. According to freecycle.org, every item posted must be free, legal, and appropriate for all ages.

If you want to find a new home for an old item or are seeking something, go online and subscribe to The Freecycle Network group in your area at no charge. Once you've found a taker—or found the item you're looking for—arrange a time and place to complete the transaction. Usually, the taker will pick up the free item. (A local volunteer moderates each group.) Freecycle members reuse items rather than throwing them away, which keeps approximately 300 tons out of landfills each day.

155 RESURRECT A BOX

Don't toss cardboard boxes. Save them until you need them. If you don't have the space to store made-up boxes, slit the tape along the bottom seams and fold the box flat. It takes only a moment and a few feet of packing tape to reconstruct a box when the need arises. If you don't have a need for the boxes, give them to someone who does. Make donations to charities for reuse or to schools for creative and educational purposes. (See "Donate Old Items," below.)

Corrugated cardboard is highly recyclable. Recycling reduces the need for new paper from virgin pulp, which in turn decreases the amount of pollution generated by paper production. It also reduces demands on landfills and incinerators. Most municipalities have facilities set up for recycling corrugated cardboard, along with newspaper. Call the local recycling office for details.

Recycle one ton of corrugated cardboard and you save 17 trees, 7,000 gallons of water, and 11 barrels of oil, and you reduce landfill by 3 cubic yards.

156 DONATE OLD ITEMS

If you've got old items—clothes, toys, furniture, housewares, and the like—don't toss them in the trash. Donate them. Give the computer desk to a college kid. Give your old chair to an antique shop, which may reupholster it and resell it. Give gently used clothes and other items to a service such as Goodwill or the Salvation Army. By extending the life of an item, you'll do your part to save the environment by keeping it out of our landfills.

157 TRY A SWAP SITE

Americans buy things. Then, we buy more things, while our previous purchases collect dust in closets, on bookshelves, and in toolboxes. An online swap site, such as switchplanet.com, swapstyle.com, or paperbackswap.com, is a great way to get rid of clothes, CDs, DVDs, toys, and other items you no longer want or need—and find items you desire. It's pretty simple, too. Sign up, list your items, make a wish list, and start swapping. On some sites, each time you send an item, you receive credits, or points, that you can use to request an item from other members. On other sites, you have to find somebody who has something you want and come up with something they want in return. (Remember trading baseball cards as a child?) Membership to swap sites is often free, and your only cost is mailing the items.

When you swap instead of shop, you reduce environmental waste and help others fill a need—and you'll save money and have access to truly unique items at the same time.

158 BUY CLOTHES SECONDHAND

Everyone wants to look good. You don't have to shop exclusively at couturiers and trendy boutiques to make that happen. The next time you're planning on expanding your wardrobe, reduce waste and the consumption of resources by shopping for secondhand clothes. It's also a way to avoid supporting sweatshops, whose labor is behind much of the clothing—often made from petroleum-based fabrics—sold today. Don't feel like leaving the house? Try eBay and Craigslist. They are great places to look for vintage T-shirts, stylish shoes, and every other sartorial item you can imagine.

159 RESTORE OLD FURNITURE

Your home isn't a museum, but you can preserve your grandfather clock or grand piano in much the same way a museum goes about caring for its collection. Furniture that's worn, scratched, cracked, or dented needn't be trashed. Restoring furniture rather than buying new saves landfill space and resources. This green effort will help you save some green (money, that is), too.

A bit of cleaning, sanding, gluing, staining, or polishing can prolong the life of this rocking chair and other pieces of furniture.

160 RECYCLE BUILDING MATERIALS

More than 100 million tons of construction and demolition waste is generated in the United States each year. When homes are built, renovated, or demolished, most of this debris (including gypsum drywall, concrete, and wood) finds its way into our landfills. It doesn't have to. Gypsum drywall, also known as wallboard, can be salvaged and reused to make new drywall. It can also be used as an ingredient in cement or even fertilizer. Recycled concrete can be ground and used for backfill or road base. Recycled lumber can be used to create anything from a kitchen cabinet to a deck—and it saves trees in the process. The ReUse People, a California-based nonprofit organization, makes the most of these cost-efficient, environmentally friendly practices. Instead of demolishing homes, the company "deconstructs" them, salvaging up to 85 percent of the building. Deconstruction is the dismantling of a structure and the salvaging of building materials, sinks, windows, and everything else that is usable. The salvaged items are sold at discounted prices or donated to nonprofit organizations, including Habitat for Humanity.

161 BUY A USED CAR

Sure, the lure of the new-car smell is strong. But buying a used car is a great way of recycling. It decreases the amount of natural materials and energy consumed to build new vehicles. (A car's manufacturing stage is responsible for roughly 10 to 20 percent of its total energy consumption and related emissions.) New cars depreciate in value quickly, so purchasing a previously owned vehicle is an economical move that allows you to take advantage of the depreciation hit incurred by the original owner.

Consumer Reports publishes lists of the best used-car choices, which can help you find a reliable, fuel-efficient car that will provide years of service. You can also check out used listings on cars.com, autotrader.com, and other Web sites. If you're not ready to buy an expensive hybrid car, buying used is the way to go.

Oh, by the way, that new-car smell comes from volatile organic compounds that are emitted by interior fabrics and plastics.

Buying a used car is a form of recycling. It's also an excellent opportunity to get a make and model you probably wouldn't be able to purchase new.

Make sure items are sorted properly. Contact your local recycling service to find out how it sorts its paper, plastics, and other recyclable items.

162 RECYCLE AT THE OFFICE

If your company doesn't already have a recycling center, set one up. Get a manager's approval, of course! First, determine what to recycle. Make it easy by starting with the basics, such as paper, bottles, and cans. Next, decide how to sort and collect the recyclables. Small bins are a good option. Put them in spots that will discourage coworkers from tossing items into the garbage. (If an employee uses lots of paper, putting a small recycling bin near his desk will help save resources.) Then, figure out how to get the items to the recycling center. A collection agency is the easiest solution, though it probably charges. The best bet, especially if you don't work for a large company, may be to have staff members make regular trips to a nearby center, perhaps on a rotating basis. Be prepared for coworkers who don't want the recycling system and won't be 100 percent supportive of your actions; ask for input and implement suggestions that would improve the program. Finally, promote the system in e-mails and at staff meetings, without nagging or being preachy. (At paperrecycles.org you can create a recycling poster customized for your office.)

163 EXTEND YOUR THINNER

Turpentine, paint thinner, and mineral spirits, commonly used for cleaning paint brushes, are toxic, carcinogenic, and potential water pollutants. Use with caution, including plenty of ventilation. Avoid skin contact and wear safety glasses. Once used, pour the dirty solvent into a glass jar. Label the jar. Within a week or two, the solids in the used solvent will fall to the bottom of the jar. Pour the clean solvent into its original container for future use. Save the jar to repeat the process, or discard at a hazardous-waste collection site.

164 RECYCLE BOTTLES AND CANS

One of the easiest ways to help sustain the environment is to recycle those plastic water bottles, aluminum soda cans, and glass wine bottles. Recycling bottles and cans reduces our reliance on landfills and incinerators, and conserves resources by reducing the need for raw materials. Recycled plastics may go back into making new bottles or be used in the manufacture of a product, such as a drainpipe or fiber for carpet and clothing, that has a longer life. Recycling aluminum saves 95 percent of the energy needed to produce new aluminum from raw materials. Glass, like aluminum, can be reused for its original purpose, and using recycled glass to make new glass bottles extends the life of plant equipment. Do your part to turn materials that would otherwise become waste into valuable resources. Depending on where you live, you may even be able to get some cash back for your recycled bottles and cans through a buy-back or a deposit/refund program.

Recycling protects our health and the environment when harmful substances are removed from the waste stream.

"You must be the change you wish to see in the world."
— Mahatma Gandhi

The United States throws out nearly 180,000 tons of batteries every year. Use rechargeables if possible.

165 GUILT-FREE BATTERY DISPOSAL

What to do with batteries when they give out is a confusing issue. And for good reason: new types of batteries are constantly being introduced as old ones are phased out; the content of batteries we think we know often changes; and rules about what needs to be recycled change, too. The common alkaline battery, for example, contains far less mercury, a highly toxic metal, than it did 10 years ago. Some states no longer require them to be recycled.

Nevertheless, a good general rule is to recycle all batteries. California, which recently banned the disposal of all batteries in the trash, has initiated a recycling program that picks up batteries (along with fluorescent bulbs) from your house. If you live elsewhere, many office-supply and electronics stores will accept some types of batteries for recycling. For battery collection sites in your locale, check out the Earth 911 Web site at earth911.org. For batteries that are not accepted by drop-off sites, you'll have to wait for a hazardous-waste collection day in your area or track down a hazardous-waste collection facility.

An easier way to recycle batteries, as well as electronic devices such as cell phones, calculators, and laptops, is to order a Big Green Box from biggreenbox.com. The box, which has a 40-pound capacity, costs about $60 and includes all shipping and disposal costs.

166 RECYCLE OR REFILL

A printer cartridge that's out of ink or toner is *not* broken, yet nearly three-quarters of used cartridges get tossed in the trash. To keep that plastic and metal out of landfills, recycle those cartridges. Or, better yet, refill them. More than 25 million cartridges go to landfills each month. Each recycled cartridge stays out of the landfill—and conserves about a half gallon of oil compared with manufacturing a new one. Some businesses, including Staples and Office Depot, accept cartridges for recycling.

Certain companies make it easy to return and recycle printing products through the mail, providing postage-paid, preaddressed labels or envelopes for returning used cartridges. In 2006, for example, more than 30 million cartridges were returned worldwide through the HP Planet Partners program, representing a weight of almost 32 million pounds. Another option is to find a store, such as Cartridge World, in your area that will refill your cartridges. You may even be able to refill them yourself. It saves money—and trips to the store.

Got the itch to shop? Thrift shops and garage sales are a fun way to do it without spending a lot. Even better, it's a way to consume without using up resources.

167 BUY GENTLY USED

Do your shopping at all manner of traditional "twice-is-nice" outlets, including garage sales, flea markets, secondhand shops, Goodwill stores, and many more. Check out the classified ads in your local newspaper, too. In addition to reducing the U.S. trade imbalance, you'll be saving the energy required to manufacture and ship new items. Save even more energy by shopping at online sites, such as eBay (ebay.com) and Craigslist (craigslist.com).

168 ORGANIZE A SPORTS SWAP

There's no need to hoard all those outgrown skates and old soccer balls. Set up a sports swap in your neighborhood. (Towns, PTAs, and local athletic organizations often arrange swaps.) Sport swaps are a good way to reduce waste, save money, and meet folks with similar interests. Display your new equipment or used equipment that's still in good condition; check out what others have to offer; and make a deal.

A good time to stage a sports-equipment swap is on a day kids register for a particular sport. Swap items include skis, golf clubs, skates, baseball bats and gloves, tennis rackets, bicycles, cleats, camping gear, inline skates, and footballs.

169 RECYCLE SHINGLES

Our landfills are piled high with old asphalt shingles, which are the most common type of roofing material used in both new homes and roof replacements. According to the Environmental Protection Agency, roof installation is estimated to generate 7 to 10 million tons of asphalt-shingle waste annually. But in some states there is a market for old asphalt shingles—or there may be a market for them on the horizon. In Missouri, for example, tear-off shingles that have been removed from the rooftops of homes and commercial buildings are used in the asphalt mix that is used in road construction projects.

When companies recycle old shingles into paving material for roads and parking lots, it's a potential win-win-win situation: roofers reduce their waste costs; pavement contractors reduce their material costs; and we reduce our landfill waste. (Approximately 150,000 tons of roofing materials are dumped in Missouri landfills each year.) If you're replacing an asphalt roof, see if a recycler in your area will take your old shingles. For more information, including environmental concerns with regard to asbestos, visit shinglerecycling.org.

170 DON'T BAG THE GRASS

Keep the rakes and bags in the garage. Leave grass clippings where they fall. Much of what goes into landfills is yard waste, so this practice will help the environment and help your lawn stay green. Clippings, which are 75 to 85 percent water, provide moisture and reduce the need for adding fertilizer because they add nitrogen to the soil as they decompose. Leaving clippings on the lawn returns nitrogen and other nutrients (phosphorus and potassium) to the soil. Clippings also act as a light mulch that helps to conserve soil moisture. If the clippings are too long to leave on the lawn, add them to your compost pile.

171 RECYCLE MOTOR OIL

Many motorists change their own oil. If you're one of them, don't toss the used motor oil into the trash or down the sewer or dump it on the ground. It's a crime, and it's an easy way to contaminate water supplies and harm animals. Carefully pour the used oil in a clean plastic container with a tight lid and take it to a collection center (often a gas station or auto-parts store) for proper recycling. Do not mix other liquids, such as gasoline, transmission fluid, or antifreeze, with the used motor oil. And don't forget that automobiles are not the only source of recycled oil. Outdoor power equipment, including mowers and lawn tractors, produce plenty of recyclable oil. According to the Environmental Protection Agency, if all do-it-yourself oil changers recycled their used oil, the United States would save 1.3 million barrels of this valuable resource each day!

Use commercially available oil-collection containers to help conserve every drop and make recycling easier.

172 GO FOR RECYCLED CONTENT

The next time you're shopping for toilet paper, tissues, paper towels, printer paper, wrapping paper, greeting cards, and other paper products—including books and magazines—look for the recycling symbol. Each time you purchase products made out of recycled paper—the higher the percentage of post-consumer recycled content, the better—you'll help conserve a surprising amount of resources. According to the William J. Clinton Foundation, if every household in the United States replaced one box of 85-sheet virgin fiber facial tissues with 100 percent recycled ones, we could save 87,700 trees, 226,500 cubic feet of landfill space, and 31 million gallons of water and avoid 5,300 pounds of pollution.

One valuable source for recycled paper products is Seventh Generation (seventhgeneration.com).

173 DON'T TOSS SCRAP METAL

From car batteries and clothes hangers to hubcaps and washing machines, many items in the garage and around the house are made from scrap metal. When it's time to get rid of these items, don't add them to the nearest landfill. Remove as much of the nonmetal materials (rubber wheels, wooden handles, and so on) as possible; responsibly dispose of any oil and gasoline; and recycle the scrap metal at your local recycling center. Recycled steel, for instance, is used in the manufacture of cars, bikes, and appliances. Soda cans, gutters, and siding are just a few items made from recycled aluminum. Recycling centers may not accept certain items because they often have hazardous components and require special handling. In that case, consider taking items to a local scrap-metal dealer. Many dealers will pay you for the metals.

Much less energy is required to make metal from scrap, such as old appliances and cars, than from ore—and at much less cost to the environment.

174 BUY USED BOOKS

It's hard to resist buying a good book, but it doesn't have to be a *new* good book. Buying a used book minimizes waste and maximizes use. Used books, which can be found at book fairs, library book sales, thrift stores, garage sales, and online, save trees and landfill space. They are less expensive, too. If you can resist the temptation of buying the latest Dean Koontz thriller or James Patterson mystery the day it's released, you can cut your carbon footprint.

Don't feel guilty about buying the occasional new book—supporting writers, publishers, and independent bookstores is a good thing. But don't let the book collect dust on a shelf. When you're finished reading it, pass it along. Keeping books circulating saves valuable resources.

Many books that are no longer in print can be found at book fairs and secondhand outlets.

175 RECYCLE OR REUSE CARPETS

In 2002, the carpet industry, government agencies, and other organizations established an agreement to increase the amount of recycling and reuse of post-consumer carpet over a 10-year time frame. The goal is to divert 40 percent of waste carpet from landfills by 2012. (For more information on the initiative, visit carpetrecovery.org.)

More than 5 billion pounds of carpet were discarded in 2007, and most of that went to landfills. When carpet is recycled, it reduces waste and recovers valuable resources. Your local recycling center may not accept carpets, which are bulky and difficult to handle. So how about giving them a second life? Cut them into small pieces and make area rugs. Donate them to an animal shelter that can use them to line cages. Wrap them around pieces of wood and create scratching posts for kittens. Use them in the garden as mulch or between rows of plants to prevent weeds.

CHAPTER 6

Green Cleaning

*I*f cleanliness is next to godliness, we ought to at least clean in nontoxic and environmentally friendly ways. In this chapter, you'll find out how to make the inside and outside of your home sparkle without having to resort to harmful chemicals.

CONTENTS

MAKE A CLEAN SWEEP

176

When possible, use a broom or carpet sweeper instead of a vacuum. Vacuums use energy and end up in landfills all too quickly. Brooms allow quick and easy cleanup, without disturbing the peace. Carpet sweepers avoid the need for a dustpan and work well on low-pile carpeting as well as hard floors. Outside, save water by using a push broom instead of a hose to clean off your driveway.

177 MICROFIBER MAGIC

Replace sponges, disposable dusting cloths, and paper towels with microfiber cloths. Microfiber's scrubbing power means you can avoid using harsh chemicals to clean, and fewer harsh chemicals means less pollution to your home and the environment. Because microfiber cloths can be washed hundreds of times, you save resources by purchasing and throwing out fewer disposable products. Another benefit is that microfiber dries quickly and is less likely to harbor bacteria than sponges.

178 SHINE WITH VINEGAR

Fancy blue glass cleaners are unnecessary. Save the burden on the planet—and your health—by making your own cleaner at home with one part white vinegar and one part water. You may need to wash your windows with soap and water before using vinegar for the first time because conventional cleaners leave a waxy film. Once the film is gone, vinegar is all you need. Use a squeegee instead of paper towels to save even more resources.

Distilled white vinegar is one of many inexpensive, versatile, green cleaning supplies. It's a mild acid that readily cleans glass, dissolves soap scum, and disinfects surfaces.

179 TOSS YOUR SOFTENER

Fabric softeners—both liquids and dryer sheets—contain a surprising amount of chemicals that can be toxic to you and the environment. And let's not forget to mention all the energy used to manufacture, pack, and ship them. A quarter cup of white vinegar added during the rinse cycle will keep clothes just as soft. If you miss the nice scent, put a few drops of essential oil on a washcloth and throw it in the dryer with your clothes.

180 CHOOSE A GREEN SERVICE

When hiring a housekeeping or janitorial service for your home or business, look for one that uses eco-friendly cleaning supplies. Some services already offer a "green" package, and others are willing to use the cleaning products you provide. If a company doesn't offer green services, ask to speak to a manager and request that the company consider offering it in the future.

181 AVOID DRY-CLEANING

Most dry-cleaning facilities in the United States use the solvent percloroethylene ("perc" for short). Chronic exposure can cause damage to the nervous system, liver, and kidneys. The Environmental Protection Agency lists it as a potential carcinogen and a hazardous air pollutant.

Your alternatives? Many "dry clean only" garments can be successfully hand-washed in cold water with a mild soap and then air-dried by laying them on a rack. But this is a gamble because water may damage the fabric or cause shrinkage or color loss. Wearing suitable undergarments under "dry clean only" garments will also reduce cleaning frequency.

If you don't dare hand-wash, there are three new types of dry-cleaning solvents that are being billed as much less toxic. They are liquid carbon dioxide, silicone-based cleaning, and "wet cleaning" (which uses a small amount of water). They appear safer for your health and the planet, but like any new technology, it will be years before all of the risks are known.

182 NONTOXIC OVEN CLEANER

Avoid highly toxic oven cleaners and save money by using baking soda to clean your oven. Make a paste of baking soda and water and spread it thickly over the walls and bottom of the oven. Let it sit overnight. The grime should be soft enough the next day that it can be wiped out. Another chemical-free way to remove grime is a vapor steam cleaner.

To minimize baked-on spills, line your oven with aluminum foil. Whenever possible use covers or foil on your dishes too. Wipe down your oven after each use, while it is still warm (but not hot).

Green cleaning methods, such as this one, work just as well as more caustic, commercial products, but they do require more time.

183 SMARTER CARPET CLEANING

Carpets can be a haven for dust mites, mold, and toxins, so it's essential to keep them clean. Prevention is your best green method. Stop dirt at the door by using extensive door mats, both inside and outside each entrance to your home. And have everyone remove their shoes upon entering.

Depending on the number of people and pets in your home, you should probably vacuum high-traffic areas several times a week. Treat stains immediately as they happen—try vinegar or club soda first. If they don't work, try dish soap, and then rinse well and dry thoroughly by blotting.

Carpets should be deep-cleaned every two to five years. If you do it yourself, use a nontoxic cleaner formulated especially for carpets. Use the smallest amount of soap possible, and pay special attention to the rinse procedure because any soap residue left in the carpets will attract dirt.

If you hire a service, ask them to use a nontoxic soap or have them clean with just hot water—many carpet-cleaning companies now offer a green option in their list of resources. Carpets should be lightly damp, not soaked, when the cleaning is complete—they need to dry within 24 hours or mold can start to grow. Keep air circulating with a fan to promote drying. Avoid using any stain-fighting treatment.

184 WORK UP A HEAD OF STEAM

Steam cleaners are a truly ideal green cleaning product. They clean and disinfect with minimal effort and no chemicals. The only drawbacks are that they do use quite a bit of energy (about the same as a vacuum), and the high-quality ones are expensive (about $500 to $2,000). But if you have allergies or multiple chemical sensitivity, you should seriously consider one. A steam cleaner works great on showers, ovens, upholstery, countertops, bare floors, and more—and it kills bacteria, mold, and dust mites.

Look for a "vapor" steam cleaner that produces "dry steam." Ones that have a boiler temperature of at least 245 degrees and a warranty on the boiler of at least three years are best. For the ultimate in convenience, choose one that will run at least an hour before it needs refilling.

"Water and air, the two essential fluids on which all life depends, have become global garbage cans."
— Jacques Cousteau

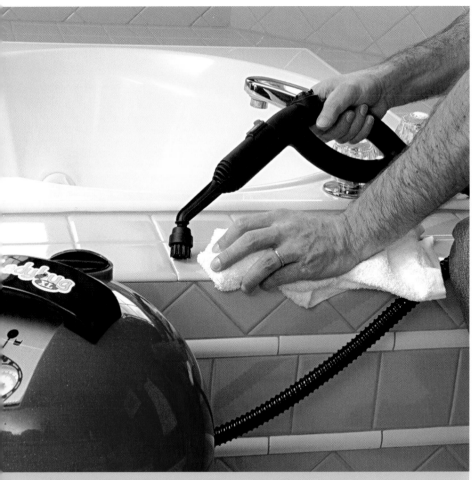

Steam cleaners come with multiple attachments for cleaning different surfaces, including a floor mop, window squeegee, and brush attachment (shown) for tough jobs, such as stained tiled grout.

Automatic dishwashing detergents made from plant oils are just as effective as those made from petroleum—and they're much healthier for you, your family, and the environment.

185 PLANT-BASED IS BETTER

When selecting cleaning products, look for ones that use plant-based ingredients, not petroleum-based ones. Petroleum is a nonrenewable resource that is energy intensive and causes pollution during extraction and refining. Many petroleum products are proven or suspected health hazards and are best avoided in the home. Most cleaning products are still petroleum-based, so look for "plant-based" specified clearly on the label.

186 DISHWASHER POWDER RECIPE

The hot temperatures of dishwashers vaporize toxins in commercial dishwashing detergents, such as chlorine, phosphates, and antibacterials. Avoid the problem by mixing your own low-cost powder.

¼ cup citric acid
1½ cups borax
15 drops essential oil (optional)

Put all ingredients in a plastic container with a tight-fitting lid and shake well. Use about 1 tablespoon per load. Shake each time before using. If you have particularly hard water, increase the amount you use with each load. You may need to prerinse your dishes because it's not quite as effective on baked-on food.

The key ingredient, citric acid (also called sour salt), can be purchased in bulk online. (See "Resources," starting on page 246.) You may also be able to find it at places that sell canning supplies. Make a big batch because this recipe also makes a great scouring powder for tubs, sinks, and countertops.

187 NONTOXIC SPRAY CLEANER

Make your own all-purpose spray cleaner at home and avoid the chemicals, packaging, and shipping that go into store-bought cleaners.

7 tsp. borax
hot water
¼ tsp. nontoxic dish soap

Add the borax and hot water to a 16-ounce spray bottle; shake until the borax is dissolved; and then add soap. Spray on surfaces; wait half a minute; and then wipe off.

188 NATURAL LAUNDRY DETERGENT

Laundry detergent is extremely heavy and therefore energy-intensive to ship. Reduce your carbon footprint by making your own with natural, nontoxic ingredients.

2 tbsp. liquid soap
1 tbsp. washing soda
¼ cup vinegar

Add liquid soap and washing soda to the washing machine as it fills. Add vinegar to the rinse cycle. Use oxygen bleach to whiten whites.

Eco-friendly cleaners can be made from scratch or purchased at many health-food stores and supermarkets.

189 FRESHER AIR FRESHENERS

Conventional air fresheners use chemicals that pollute the environment and are questionable for human health. Make your own eco-friendly spray by adding 8 to 12 drops of essential oil to a fine-mist spray bottle filled with distilled water. Essential oils that work nicely are lemon, lavender, peppermint, sweet rosemary, or cedarwood. Clay pot diffusers also work well. The essential oil permeates the clay container's walls. Another air-freshening option is to simmer fresh herbs or citrus peels in a pot of water on your stove.

To deodorize just about anything, use baking soda alone or with a few drops of natural essential oil, such as lemon or eucalyptus. You will need to add fresh oil every few days.

190 DEODORIZE WITH BAKING SODA

Baking soda is a natural, nontoxic mineral with myriad green cleaning uses. One of its best features is its ability to remove odors. So get rid of smelly candles and chemical air fresheners and stick with the basics instead. Some ideas:

- **Sprinkle in the diaper pail** daily.
- **Put in a box** on a shelf to keep the bathroom smelling fresh.
- **Sprinkle on pet beds** or carpets; let sit for hours; and then vacuum.
- **Sprinkle in your kitchen** garbage can or compost bin daily.
- **Cover the bottom** of the kitty litter box.
- **Add half a cup** to your wash cycle to absorb odors from clothes.
- **Sprinkle in shoes** and boots and let sit overnight.

191 USE FEWER PAPER TOWELS

There are plenty of options out there that can help you reduce your usage of paper towels. They are easy to reach for, but you can save trees and limit manufacturing and shipping costs by using less. Some easy substitutions:

• **Spills:** Use a squeegee to scrape spills into a dust pan.

• **Spills:** Use a sponge to absorb the liquid, and then wring it out into a container. For big jobs use a sponge mop and bucket.

• **Hands:** Keep a hand towel near all sinks (or let hands air-dry).

• **Windows:** Use a squeegee or sponge to clean.

• **Counters:** Use a sponge, cotton rag, or microfiber cloth to clean counters and other surfaces.

Don't forget to disinfect sponges and towels to avoid spreading germs. Wash cloths and towels in the washing machine frequently, and disinfect sponges in the microwave. (Put a soaking wet sponge in and cook on high for three minutes.)

A squeegee is just one alternative to using paper towels.

192 SAY UH-UH TO ANTIBACTERIALS

The products you use for washing dishes end up in our groundwater. Preserve local water quality by selecting a non-toxic dish soap. Avoid ones that say "antibacterial"—antibacterial agents may help create antibiotic-resistant "superbugs," and the American Medical Association advises against them. And being "antibacterial" does not mean they clean any better. For pots and pans with heavy grime, soak them in hot water with a few tablespoons of baking soda. If you use a dishwasher, save energy and water by not prerinsing dishes, running only full loads, and selecting a short cycle with no-heat dry.

193 GREENER FLOOR CARE

As with carpets, prevention is the best green care for hard-surface floors such as wood and tile. The cleaner you keep them, the less need you'll have for harsh chemicals. Use door mats and sweep or dust-mop frequently. (Microfiber dust mops work great, and the detachable pad can be washed hundreds of times.) Limit vacuuming because it uses electricity.

Avoid wet-mopping hardwood, laminate, bamboo, or linoleum because large amounts of water can damage them. Damp-mop them instead using a microfiber mop or sponge mop that has been well wrung out. Use a 50/50 mix of white vinegar and water for light cleaning, and use a nontoxic, plant-oil-based floor cleaner for heavier grime. Use the same cleaners for tile, stone, rubber, vinyl, and concrete, but because they are fairly impervious to water, you can wet-mop instead of damp-mop.

Use a microfiber mop cover along with a plant-oil-based cleaner to make floors sparkle without toxins.

194 GENTLER FURNITURE CARE

Try the following solutions:

• **White haze and drink rings:** These rings are caused by moisture getting into the finish and not being able to evaporate. Rub any sort of oil (such as olive oil or coconut oil) into the ring and let it sit until whiteness disappears, and then wipe off with a dry cloth.

• **Stickers:** To remove stickers or paper stuck to a wood surface, cover with any oil (such as olive oil), and let it sit until it is saturated; then gently rub with a soft cloth until it is removed.

• **Polish:** Opt for waxes made without petroleum-based solvents. Use coasters and felt pads to prevent scratches.

195 REMOVE STAINS NATURALLY

Most clothing stains can be removed without harsh petroleum-based removers by using these tips:

• **Rinse protein stains** (egg, milk, urine, feces, vomit, blood) under cold running water while scrubbing gently. If the stain doesn't come right out, soak it in cold water.

• **Pretreat oil-based stains** (cooking oil, food grease, motor oil) by applying a liquid soap directly to the stain and rubbing gently. Rinse with hot water, and then wash in hot water.

• **Soak tannin stains** (red wine, tea, coffee, juice, ketchup, soft drinks) for 30 minutes with a teaspoon of liquid detergent per half gallon of water.

• **Soak the garment** in oxygen bleach if the above options don't work.

• **Don't put the item in the dryer** unless you're sure the stain is gone because the heat will set the stain.

196 KEEP SILVER SHINING

This is an easy and eco-friendly way to make silver-plated tableware shine.

1. Place a sheet of aluminum foil at the bottom of a Pyrex baking dish, and then lay the silverware on top.

2. Sprinkle a teaspoon of salt and several tablespoons of baking soda over the silverware.

3. Pour boiling water into the dish, and let it sit for a minute.

4. Remove each piece and polish with a soft cloth.

This method eliminates the need for noxious polishes, but it does release hydrogen sulfide gas, so do it in a well-ventilated area.

197 GREENER CAR WASHING

Washing a car wastes water and sends chemical-filled soap into the ecosystem. Try the following tips to help minimize your impact:

- **Always pull your car onto grass** or gravel before washing.
- **Use a nontoxic soap,** but only half the recommended amount.
- **Put a shutoff valve** or spray nozzle on the end of your hose so you can easily turn it off when you're not using it.
- **Use a paste of baking soda** and dish soap to remove bugs and tar.
- **Use rubber floor mats** inside your car to minimize carpet cleaning.

198 CHOOSE CONCENTRATE

Whenever possible buy either concentrated liquids or powder versions of cleaning products that give you the most number of uses per ounce. Concentrated formulas cost less to ship and use less packaging than their unconcentrated counterparts. Be careful not to negate all the good things about concentrated products by using too much. Follow the manufacturer's instructions, and keep a measuring spoon or cup handy. You might even try using less than the manufacturer recommends—sometimes half the amount works just as well.

199 WASH WITH WATER POWER

Cleaning your home's exterior is never an easy task and inevitably uses a lot of water. Choose low-maintenance materials whenever possible to avoid frequent cleaning. When you do need to clean your siding, deck, or driveway, renting a power washer can help you get the job done without toxic chemicals. Often just the pressure of the water is enough to clean a surface. If you do need to use soap, choose a nontoxic, biodegradable soap to minimize impact on the environment. Avoid harsh chemicals.

Be aware that too much pressure can damage what you're cleaning. Adjust the nozzle to the lowest pressure, and test in an inconspicuous area first. Avoid power-washing delicate materials such as stucco. Always spray your roof or walls from above so that water doesn't seep in under the shingles or siding. For stains, try scrubbing with oxygen bleach or washing soda. Use borax in your cleaning solution to help prevent mold.

CHAPTER 7

Reducing Pollution

Most of us think of pollution on an industrial scale: belching smoke stacks, brown fields, and beaches and birds coated with crude oil. But like most things, pollution begins at home. Here are some small things you can do to turn the tide.

CONTENTS

LET THERE BE BIRDS

Here's an idea that's for the birds…literally. Buy a birdhouse (or build your own) and invite a natural form of insect control into your yard. You'll be able to say bye-bye to most harmful pesticides and let birds do the work for you. Plus, you'll get to enjoy the sights and sounds of your feathered friends, and you may stimulate a child's interest in nature.

Not all birds use a birdhouse, or nest box, but those that do include bluebirds, wrens, and chickadees.

Redwood and cedar are good, rot-resistant building materials. (You can also make a house out of a gourd.) Make sure it has a slanted, overhanging roof (to keep away rain and stalking predators) and a hinged top or side (for cleaning out old nests). Other design details of your birdhouse—including size of the box and diameter of the entry hole—may depend on what species you're trying to attract. Use a nontoxic finish or leave it natural. Locate it out of the reach of cats and other predators. A birdhouse mounted on a metal pole is less vulnerable to predators than a house mounted to a tree trunk or hung from a limb.

201 BE RID OF MOSQUITOES

Mosquitoes are, in many regions, the insect that is the most annoying. They are also bearers of diseases such as West Nile fever. For decades, homeowners who enjoy backyard entertaining have tried insecticides, repellents, and electric insect-killing machines with mixed success—some of which come with health risks of their own.

Here are some natural ways to defend yourself without resorting to the use of toxic chemicals:

• **Use a natural mosquito-repelling oil,** such as citronella, lemon eucalyptus, rosemary, peppermint, and cedar. Reapply at least every two hours.

• **Control the environment.** Moisture, CO_2, dark colors, and fragrances, found in everything from perfumes to fabric softeners, are attractants. So keep your entertaining area dry for your dinner party, don't light your fireplace when mosquitoes are most active (dawn and dusk), wear light-colored clothing, and keep your body and clothing fragrance free.

• **Avoid being a target.** Lactic acid, produced when you've been working out, is an attractant, so cool down before heading outside.

• **Use a misting fan** in hot weather. These units produce a light fog that causes temperatures to drop and deters insects at the same time. Many units can be used to disperse natural insect repellents, including pyrethrum and citronella as well.

• **Use screening,** another non-toxic way to keep mosquitoes at bay. In addition to conventional aluminum screening, which can be recycled, consider mosquito netting. It can be installed as curtains around open porches or detached structures, including gazebos.

• **Use insect traps** that work on mosquitoes but not on beneficial insects. One type uses propane to produce CO_2 that the pests mistake for breath. When they arrive at the device, usually placed well away from the entertaining area, they're vacuumed into a net where they dehydrate and die.

This screened pavilion allows homeowners to enjoy their wooded setting even during the high season for mosquitoes.

202 TURN OFF LIGHT POLLUTION

Light itself can pollute in several ways. Glare, for example, can cause unsafe conditions for visitors unfamiliar with your property. Reduce it by lowering wattage, and redirecting fixtures and diffusers. "Light trespass," another type of light pollution, is when your lighting intrudes upon a nearby property, such as when a floodlight shines into a neighbor's window. Redirecting fixtures or using shields can help. "Sky glow" happens when light is wastefully shined into the night sky and is one of the reasons it's difficult to see stars in many locations. Many lighting manufacturers are designing shades into their products to solve the problem. Shades can also be installed on existing fixtures.

Many companies have introduced "dark sky" shield accessories to help

Newly designed lights for entryways put light only where you need it. They won't contribute to nighttime light pollution or be an annoyance to your neighbors.

avoid night-sky pollution and to enable compliance with night-sky protection ordinances that are popping up around the country.

203 SAY NO TO POISONS

Few of us like killing animals, even pests, but sometimes there's no choice. For rodents, choose traps that kill quickly and don't use poisons that can come back to haunt us. Standard spring-action traps, baited with peanut butter or cheese for mice and peanut butter or bacon for rats, are highly effective. Place the traps unset in areas where activity is suspected as a way to acclimate rodents to the traps. Use small amounts of bait that the animal must struggle to get.

Place traps along walls, the path rodents prefer, with the baited end of the trap against the wall. Check traps daily and wear gloves when disposing of them. (For a more humane and labor-intensive approach, see "Catch and Release" on page 141.)

A second, nontoxic approach to a pest-free home is to repel rather than poison unwanted visitors. Repellents typically seek out the animals' Achilles' heel. Rat and mouse repellents, for example, play to the animal's highly developed sense of smell or hearing. Compounds with sulfur have proven highly effective in reducing rat and mouse activity in treated buildings and garbage collection areas.

Ultrasonic sound wave emitters, found in every hardware store, purport to work in a similar way for a variety of pests—but with sound instead of odor. Test results are mixed for these devices, with some users saying you must place one in every room for them to be effective.

204 CANDLELIGHT WITHOUT THE VOCS

Americans love lighting candles. According to the National Candle Association, candles are used in 7 out of 10 U.S. households. Unfortunately, most scented candles are made from paraffin wax, a petroleum byproduct. If you can't resist the ambiance candles provide, try 100 percent beeswax or soy candles instead. Beeswax and soy wax are biodegradable, renewable resources. They burn cleaner and produce less black soot than paraffin wax. Plus, using soy candles is a great way to support farmers who sell soybeans.

205 HANDLING ASBESTOS

Asbestos, once billed as a marvel, has taken its place alongside lead and radon gas as one of the pollutants about which a homeowner should be concerned, but not necessarily panicked. It was commonly used in many building products through the late 1970s, including pipe and duct insulation, textured paint, patching compounds, sheet and tile flooring, furnace door gaskets, siding, roofing, and brake pads. As it has become clear that it is unhealthy to ingest or inhale asbestos dust, its uses and removal from buildings have become regulated worldwide.

If you live in a home built before 1980, it probably has one or more products that include asbestos. Here are the general guidelines for what to do about it:

• **If the material is in good condition,** it is unlikely to release fiber. Leave it in place.

• **If the material is damaged,** consult with a remediation professional about whether it makes sense to repair (seal or cover) or remove it.

• **If you're renovating your home** and likely to disturb, break apart, saw, or sand a material containing asbestos, consult with a remediation professional about removal. Check with the Environmental Protection Agency or state or local health departments for listings of licensed asbestos professionals.

Asbestos is a family of fibrous minerals with useful properties, including fire and heat resistance, and the ability to be woven. Unfortunately, its uses today have been limited because breathing or ingesting the fibers can eventually cause lung and intestinal diseases.

206 MOW WITH MUSCLE

Mowers are inherently messy contraptions. They use gasoline—a nonrenewable resource—as fuel and require regular oil changes to perform properly. Noise and emissions are unavoidable. Manufacturing an internal combustion engine is in itself highly energy intensive. If you've reduced your lawn area to something under 5,000 square feet, consider the much cleaner options of either a corded or cordless electric mower. (See "Downsize Your Lawn" on page 93.) A corded mower is limited to 100 feet from your outdoor electric outlet. A battery-powered unit is not. The latter typically has a run time of 45 to 90 minutes, depending on the height and thickness of the turf. If your lawn is smaller, try a manual push mower. It's a good workout, and the only power you'll use is your own.

Most manual push mowers are made by the American Mower Company. They have limited height adjustability, so you can't allow your lawn to get too long and still be able to mow it. If you buy a push mower, order the blade-sharpening kit, too.

207 CATCH AND RELEASE

If you don't want to kill unwanted house pests, try a more humane approach. Catching a spider in a napkin and releasing it outdoors is not much more difficult than stomping on it and cleaning up the smudge. Many humane-type rodent traps will readily catch squirrels and mice; peanut butter works well as a bait. Most traps catch one rodent at a time, but some will catch multiple animals. Wind-up traps can capture entire families of mice with just one setting, saving you time and mess. Driving to a remote area to release a trapped animal isn't recommended because the animal may not survive—and if it does, it may return. Driving also wastes gas. Contact a licensed wildlife rehabilitator, who can take the animal and help it cope with its new surroundings.

208 CHEMICAL-FREE DRAIN CLEANING

You don't need caustic chemicals to clean your household drains. For most partial stoppages, it's often enough to fill the sink or tub with water and then release the stopper. The water pressure will frequently dislodge the clog. Help the process along by using your hand as a plunger. If the drain is completely clogged, run a hose from an outdoor or indoor spigot. Remove any sprayer attachment, hold the hose in the drain hole, and have someone turn on the water full blast. The rush of the water should break up any clog.

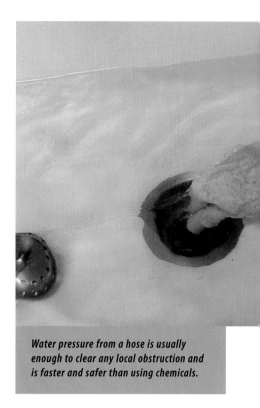

Water pressure from a hose is usually enough to clear any local obstruction and is faster and safer than using chemicals.

209 SEND INSECTS PACKING

Boric acid is a toxin-free pesticide that was discovered in the Mojave Desert in the 1920s. A white powder that's found in dozens of pest-control products today, it's safe for humans and pets—as long as it's not swallowed, inhaled, or gotten in the eyes. Boric acid affects insects' nervous systems and acts as a desiccant, drying out insects' bodies. In university trials, it has been effective with a wide range of insects, including palmetto bugs, cockroaches, carpenter ants, and termites. Sprinkle the powder where insects hang out, such as behind refrigerators, along baseboards, and under cabinets. A favorite trick of exterminators when dealing with sweet-loving ants is to mix it one to one with peanut butter or honey so the ants will bring it back to the nest. Do not apply boric acid to surfaces that may come in contact with food, and keep it away from children.

For new construction or an extensive renovation, sprinkle boric acid powder in wall voids and inside soffits to discourage insects from intruding in the first place.

210 BUY SAFER TOYS

Children lick toys. Children chew on toys. Children touch toys and then put their fingers in their mouths. These are facts of life. To keep your child safe when these events inevitably occur, stay away from toxic toys, including ones made from PVC and ones made with lead or lead paint. (In 2007, millions of toys made in China were recalled because of unsafe levels of lead paint.) Chronic exposure to toxins can lead to learning disabilities and a variety of behavioral problems.

Look for safe, fun, creative toys made in the United States; a local independent toy dealer offers unique playthings that haven't traveled thousands of miles to get to you. Wood toys—especially those made from wood certified by the Forest Stewardship Council—are safe and will last for generations. For more information about recalled toys, visit the U.S. Consumer Product Safety Commission's Web site, cpsc.gov. You can join a recall notification list and receive e-mail updates.

The simplest toy is often the best. Blocks, anyone? All your child needs is an imagination. No batteries required.

An efficient wood fire requires the placement of a large piece of firewood near the front of the grate. It helps control the fire's burn rate so it's not too fast or too slow.

211 BURN WOOD EFFICIENTLY

Wood, despite being a renewable fuel, releases carbon dioxide and other pollutants when burned. If burned in a fireplace, most of the heat goes up the flue. Warm air from inside your home often goes up the flue, too, and is replaced by cold air from the outside—making your furnace work harder.

If you burn wood regularly, do it in an eco-conscious manner. Use well-seasoned hardwood, not green wood, and burn it in an efficient wood stove, fireplace insert, or wood-burning furnace. If you see smoke while you're burning wood, it's due to an inefficient burn. Newer wood-burning appliances burn more of the gases, capturing more energy from each piece of firewood.

Choose a stove certified by the Environmental Protection Agency to ensure efficiency. Have it, along with the flue, professionally installed by a certified technician to ensure its safety and proper performance.

212 FIGHT WEEDS WITH FIRE

There are many creative methods for eliminating weeds from your garden without resorting to noxious herbicides. Organic farmers, for example, have successfully used fire to kill weeds.

"Flaming" is done with a gas torch that emits a narrow flame. Pass the clear cone of gas surrounding the flame across the foliage until it starts to wilt. Because the roots aren't injured, you will need to repeat this treatment when the foliage regrows. Eventually the weed will use up its store of food and be unable to reproduce or grow.

213 RAKE THE OLD-FASHIONED WAY

Autumn is a time for falling leaves...and screeching leaf blowers. Next time the leaves pile up, reach for a rake or broom instead of the noise-making, exhaust-emitting (if it's gas-powered), air-polluting leaf blower. Hundreds of towns in the United States and Canada, including Palo Alto, California, Evanston, Illinois, and Vancouver, British Columbia, have full or partial bans on leaf blowers—relatively small devices that pack a big polluting punch. Good old-fashioned raking may be more labor intensive, but it's a quieter way to save energy, say goodbye to exhaust fumes and debris clouds, and burn some calories. Most yards can be raked in under an hour.

Forget gas power. Forget electric power. Use human power. Your neighbors will thank you.

A rake made from bamboo—a fast-growing, renewable resource—is lightweight and easy to use; steel and plastic rakes will last longer.

214 CHANGE OIL WITH CARE

According to the Environmental Protection Agency, more fuel is spilled each year filling up garden equipment than was lost in the entire Exxon Valdez oil spill in Alaska in 1989. Spilled oil often washes into storm drains, contaminating the water supply, or seeps into the ground, contaminating the soil that feeds plants. And it doesn't take much to cause environmental harm: the motor oil from a single oil change can contaminate a million gallons of drinking water.

So the next time you're changing the oil in your car or lawn mower, do so on a flat, dry surface (a driveway or sidewalk, for example)—*not* on the lawn. Position a drip pan—one that's big enough to handle the job—under the drain plug. Use something absorbent to soak up spills immediately. (Sawdust and kitty litter work well.)

215 WEAR AN ECO-WATCH

Got the "time" to be earth friendly? If you do, consider a watch that runs on light energy or motion energy. Solar-powered watches use a solar panel beneath the dial to convert light into energy. An energy cell stores the electrical energy—it can store enough to power the watch for up to five years. (Most models have a power reserve that lasts about six months.) Sunlight and, in most cases, indoor lighting recharge the batteries.

Batteries in a motion-powered watch are recharged by the wearer's arm motion. A tiny rotor spins in response to the motion of the arm to generate electrical energy. The energy stored in a motion-powered watch can power it for days without the watch being worn.

With one of these watches on your wrist, you'll never have to buy—and dispose of—batteries again. The power supply for both watches is limitless and free. So, what time is it? Time to consider a new watch.

216 TEST ITEMS FOR LEAD

Exposure to lead is dangerous. Even tiny amounts of this toxic metal (measured in micrograms) can pose health risks, such as lower mental development, neurological damage, and hearing loss. Children, who often put things in their mouths or touch things and then put their hands in their mouths, are at a greater health risk. To protect your household, test items for lead. Paint, water, toys, jewelry, pipes, candlewicks, and lipstick are just some of the things that can be tested.

The simplest way to test for lead is to use a home test kit, which typically costs less than $20. A swab changes colors in the presence of lead on a surface. Do-it-yourself kits offer immediate results, but those results aren't going to be as accurate as a laboratory test. Kits are best used to help you determine whether further testing is necessary. If it is, have a lead inspector or risk assessor check your home, or send items to a certified laboratory. For a list of contacts or labs in your area, contact the National Lead Information Center at 800-424-LEAD.

Bat houses that are mounted on poles or buildings have higher occupancies.

217 BUILD A BAT HOUSE

Worried about breathing in the stuff you spray around the yard to ward off mosquitoes? Let bats do the work for you. According to Bat Conservation International, one bat can capture 500 to 1,000 mosquitoes in an hour. Bats also assist with the natural pollination of plants.

Bat houses are available as kits or ready-made. You can also find plans online to build your own. Spring is the best time to install a bat house. Choose a sunny location.

218 USE A SNOW SHOVEL

The tropical vacation is over. You're back home. No escaping the snow now. Instead of clearing it with a snow thrower, use a shovel. Shoveling is more laborious, sure, but it's better for the environment. A gas-powered snow thrower emits about a pound or two of carbon monoxide every hour. Next time it snows, burn some calories. Use an ergonomically designed shovel or consider a Wovel, a wheeled shovel. (See wovel.com.)

Shoveling snow cuts down on noise pollution, too. Just go slow and easy. If you have heart or back problems, shoveling is not recommended. If you're not up to the task of shoveling, hire a local teenager to do it for you.

219 TEST FOR RADON

Radon is a colorless, odorless, and tasteless gas that is derived from the radioactive decay of radium. It comes from the earth and rocks beneath homes. It is also found in some construction materials and ground water. As radon decays, the resulting particles, or "progeny," may attach to dust, become airborne, and be inhaled. Once in the lungs, radon progeny continue to emit alpha particles that can trigger cancerous cell growth. Based on studies of miners, the Environmental Protection Agency (EPA) attributes 15,000 to 20,000 lung cancer deaths per year to radon exposure, second only to smoking. In addition, preliminary tests indicate that radon and tobacco smoke are a bad combination. Smoking increases the chance of radon-induced lung cancer beyond the sum of smoking and radon risks added together. Radon has also been implicated in deaths due to other forms of cancer and leukemia. What can you do?

• **Test your home for radon.** You may do this yourself or hire a professional.

• **Fix the situation** if the test results show that the radon level is 4 picocuries per liter (pCi/L) or greater. (The average home is 1.3 pCi/L, and the average outdoor level is .4 pCi/L.)

• **Consider remediation** even if you are below the recommended level. The health risk caused by radon is not eliminated even at the recommended EPA level of 4 pCi/L.

• **Seal all cracks** and around openings for pipes and drains with caulk.

• **Cover sumps** with tight-fitting covers for sumps and other openings.

• **Hire a remediation specialist** to vent the space under the basement floor slab.

• **Increase ventilation** in crawlspaces or the basement.

• **Increase house ventilation** with a heat recovery ventilator.

220 SHOES OFF, PLEASE

Paul Simon sang about a girl who had diamonds on the soles of her shoes. The rest of us aren't so lucky. Our soles are havens for all sorts of toxins, including pesticides. To keep the dirt and grime away, consider adopting a shoes-off policy in your home, especially if you have toddlers or young children who spend a lot of time on the floor. To avoid confrontations with folks who may feel offended if they're asked to go sans shoes, you may want to have slippers available in a variety of sizes.

Leave adequate space by each door to store shoes. (If you're short on space, tiered shoe racks are available.)

221 COVER YOUR POOL

Lots of chemicals, water, and energy are used to clean and maintain swimming pools, spas, and hot tubs. The simplest way to use less of all these things is to use a tight-fitting cover. Covers reduce chemical usage by keeping out debris. They also reduce water loss—an uncovered pool can lose thousands of gallons a year through evaporation. A solar cover allows a pool to collect—and retain—heat from the sun, which means you don't have to run your pool or spa heater as often.

Most pool and spa owners use chlorine to destroy algae and bacteria. Natural, mineral-based sanitizers can do the same job, without the unhealthy side effects, including skin irritation, eye irritation, and the unpleasant chlorine smell. If you want to say goodbye to chlorinated water, see nature2.com or chlorfree.net.

222 DRIVEWAYS THAT DON'T RUN OFF

If your driveway needs replacing, consider switching to a permeable pavement. Conventional asphalt or concrete surfaces catch and funnel water—along with pesticides, oil, and other contaminants—into already overworked sewers. Permeable pavements can be made of asphalt, concrete, gravel, flagstone, and grass, and you can find them in any home center. Interlocking paving systems made of concrete or recycled plastic, use a grid system to prevent compaction and to drain the water to the underlying soil, filtering certain pollutants and replenishing underground water sources.

Another benefit of a permeable driveway with a natural land cover is that it reduces the "heat island effect." Urban and suburban areas are generally hotter than surrounding rural areas because impervious materials used in driveways, roads, buildings, and other structures absorb the sun's energy, forming "heat islands."

Real pavers—not look-alikes stamped in concrete—keep runoff from causing pollution.

> *"Pollution should never be the price of prosperity."*
> — Al Gore

223   NO-TOX TERMITE CONTROL

If you've got active termite infestation, your first instinct may be to run for the chemicals or set up the fumigation tent. Hold on. Safer alternatives are available. A baiting system may take months to wipe out a termite colony, but it doesn't require pesticides. In one popular system, termites take the bait—a fatal insect growth regulator—and spread it throughout the colony. Bait systems are installed underground and require monitoring and maintenance by a professional. Another method, though one that may be most effective if it's applied during construction, is to create physical barriers. Termites can't squeeze or chew through a coarse-sand barrier around the foundation and are unable to penetrate a stainless-steel mesh barrier around pipes and other possible entry points. Some pest-control operators apply a beneficial fungus called Bio-Blast, which isn't harmful to humans, directly onto colonies. Spot-treatment methods include applying heat or freezing the termites by injecting liquid nitrogen into wall voids.

Termites are small, but they can do big damage. They do their damage slowly, however, so you have time to formulate the best—and greenest—plan of attack.

If termite infestation is found, it's best to let a professional control it.

224 DEBUGGING WITHOUT TOXINS

Bugged by all the bugs? Don't reach for the repellents containing chemicals, such as DEET. Try safer products made from natural ingredients—herbs and essential oils—to keep the mosquitoes, flies, ants, and wasps at bay.

Peppermint, citronella, and cedar are just a few of the essential oils that can be found in nontoxic bug repellents. Rosemary oil is the featured ingredient in the Herbal Insect Repellent from Burt's Bees (burtsbees.com), and Aubrey Organics' Gone! spray (aubrey-organics.com) is a blend of herbal oils, including sage, lavender, eucalyptus, and rosemary.

You can also try making your own repellent at home, using one of the many recipes found online. (Try earth-easy.com.) A natural bug repellent does not have the "staying power" of products containing DEET, so you may have to reapply it more frequently. But it's a small price to pay to feel confident about something that you're rubbing on your skin.

225 GET UP ALL THE DUST

To minimize indoor air pollution, you'll need a vacuum that completely traps dust and dirt (and the allergens and chemical residues they contain) and prevents them from escaping back into your home. If you have allergies, asthma, or multiple chemical sensitivity, buy the best vacuum you can afford. HEPA (High Efficiency Particulate Air) filtration is an important feature to have. A vacuum with a HEPA filter can retain more than 99.9 percent of particles as small as 0.3 micrometers. (To get an idea of how small a particle that is 0.3 micrometers is, consider that a human hair is approximately 100 micrometers thick.)

Not all HEPA vacuums are equal. *Consumer Reports* found that the level of dust emissions depended as much on the vacuum design as it did the type of filtration. Look for models with a "completely sealed" HEPA system. Also look for vacuums that have earned the Carpet and Rug Institute Green Label certification. These vacuums have passed stringent tests for soil removal and dust containment.

If you have a bag vacuum, empty the bag when it gets half full—after that it starts to lose sucking power and you waste energy.

226 CLEAR THE AIR

Most of us spend at least half our lives in our homes, drawing about a dozen breaths of air in every minute. That adds up to at least 8,640 lung-fulls every day. But is that air safe? The Environmental Protection Agency doesn't think so. It lists indoor air quality as one of the five top environmental issues of our day, saying it can be 5 to 10 times more polluted than outdoor air, even in cities where air quality is poor. Common contaminants include tobacco smoke, combustion pollutants, mold, and other biological contaminants. Here are three ways to improve indoor air quality:

• **Source control:** Some controls are simply common sense, such as cleaning regularly and using a dehumidifier if necessary. Others require setting rules, such as banning smoking in your home and keeping pets properly groomed. Source control also requires maintenance of appliances, such as furnaces and vacuums.

• **Ventilation:** According to the American Society of Heating, Refrigerating and Air-Conditioning Engineers, the air in your home should be exchanged about once every three hours, or 0.35 time per hour. Ventilation strategies include opening windows, installing exhaust fans, and installing radon-mitigation systems.

• **Air cleaning:** Air cleaners work by lowering concentrations and lessening exposure. Some are built into heating systems. Others are portable, combining a blower and a filter. Air cleaners, especially those equipped with HEPA filters, are effective, but they cannot remove all pollutants. Some allergens, for example, quickly settle to the floor, where an air cleaner can't reach them. Air cleaners are best used together with source control and ventilation strategies.

CHAPTER 8

Getting Around

We've become a little crazy. Many of us will spend a half hour on a treadmill at the gym but won't walk to the grocery store. Read on for ways to "get around" that pollute less and conserve more—and are way healthier for all involved.

CONTENTS

BE A TELECOMMUTER

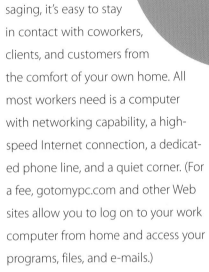

227

According to former New Jersey governor Christine Todd Whitman, America's 5 million telecommuters save about $120 million in gas costs and prevent the emission of 1.76 billion pounds of CO_2 every day. So stay home if you can. Working from home means less wasted time and traffic-related stress, too. With video conferencing, e-mailing, and instant messaging, it's easy to stay in contact with coworkers, clients, and customers from the comfort of your own home. All most workers need is a computer with networking capability, a high-speed Internet connection, a dedicated phone line, and a quiet corner. (For a fee, gotomypc.com and other Web sites allow you to log on to your work computer from home and access your programs, files, and e-mails.)

Telecommuting isn't suited to everyone, of course, but it could work if you do a lot of writing or researching or computer programming. You have to be disciplined, though—no TV watching or napping!

Telecommuting doesn't have to be a full-time commitment; the environmental impact is great when millions of people work from home only a day or two each week. Another option? Some companies allow employees to work four 10-hour days instead of five 8-hour days, which means one less gas-consuming, air-polluting commute each week.

228 RENT A GREEN CAR

Unless you live in a cave, hybrid vehicles have probably gotten your attention by this time. But who wants to have to deal with a dealer just to test-drive one?

Next time you need to rent a car, call ahead and ask your car rental company to reserve a hybrid for you. If it doesn't have one, go online and find one that does. Many rental companies offer them, and they're available for pickup at airports in many major cities.

If you can't find a hybrid at the companies you call, ask for a vehicle that's SmartWay certified. SmartWay is the Environmental Protection Agency's green vehicle ratings program. A SmartWay rating of 6 or better ensures that your rental produces fewer harmful emissions and greenhouse gases than the average vehicle. For a listing of SmartWay certified cars and their ratings, go to epa.gov/greenvehicles.

229 KEEP TIRES INFLATED

Underinflated tires require more energy because they increase "rolling resistance." The engine has to work harder and, consequently, more fuel is consumed. According to the Department of Energy, properly inflated tires can improve your gas mileage by 3.3 percent, and underinflated tires waste more than 3.5 million gallons of gas each day! Keeping your tires at the recommended PSI (pounds per square inch) creates less work for the engine, saves fuel, helps tires wear evenly and last longer, and emits fewer greenhouse gases into the atmosphere.

Check tire pressure at least once a month. The recommended tire pressure is usually found in the owner's manual or on a sticker in the doorjamb—not on the tire, which usually lists maximum pressure.

> *"Every time I see an adult on a bicycle, I no longer despair for the future of the human race."*
> *— H.G. Wells*

230 JOIN A CARPOOL

The average commute is 15 miles, which means you drive about 7,500 miles a year going to and from work in a fuel-guzzling, air-polluting vehicle. One way to burn less gas and cut back on greenhouse gases is to carpool. It's not quite as green as walking, bicycling, or taking public transportation, but it's more earth-friendly than driving alone. Try it with a co-worker or neighbor or, if you don't mind sharing a ride with a stranger, use one of the many carpooling Web sites, such as carpoolconnect.com and erideshare.com. You'll cut gas costs and save wear on your car, and you may be able to get a reduction on your car insurance, too. Another plus? Taking turns behind the wheel means you're not always the one whose stress level is elevating because of bumper-to-bumper traffic, aggressive drivers, and the other inevitable aspects of the daily commute. Only 10 percent of Americans carpool to work. If that number were to rise, our energy dependence would fall. It's happened before: during World War II, the U.S. government urged carpooling because gas was in short supply—one poster from that era stated, "When you ride alone you ride with Hitler!"

If your area has a carpool lane, also known as a high-occupancy vehicle (HOV) lane, sharing a ride to work may mean a quicker commute.

The Toyota Prius (above), the most popular hybrid, gets about 45 miles per gallon. The Toyota Camry, Honda Civic, and Ford Escape are just a few of the popular models available as a hybrid.

231 CONSIDER A HYBRID CAR

The United States consumes more than 20 million barrels of oil each day, and 40 percent of that is used by passenger vehicles. Driving gas-electric hybrid cars, which can slash fuel consumption by almost half, is one way those of us who depend on a car can use less fuel and do our part to clean the air.

The secret to a hybrid's success is that it can shut off its smaller, more efficient gas engine and run in the electric mode on batteries when traveling at slow speeds or stopped at a red light, which is when CO_2 emissions and fuel consumption are greatest. The gas engine turns a generator, which charges the batteries or directly powers the electric motor that drives the transmission. The electric motor draws energy from the batteries, but it also acts as a generator when you brake, recovering kinetic energy and storing it in the batteries through a process known as regenerative braking.

With surging oil prices (and therefore escalating prices at the gas pump), you may want to give some thought to a hybrid. An entry-level hybrid will carry a premium in its sticker price over a nonhybrid counterpart, but you may make up for the extra cost in fuel savings.

232 LIGHTEN YOUR LOAD

It shouldn't come as a surprise that the more weight you have in your car, the harder the engine has to work, which means lower gas mileage. In fact, according to the Department of Energy, an extra 100 pounds in your car reduces fuel economy by up to 2 percent. If you remove any unnecessary items and lighten the load by 100 pounds, you can save about 6¢ a gallon. Clean out your car every so often, removing any books, strollers, and sports gear. Leave only what is necessary, such as a flashlight, some tools, and a first-aid kit.

233 RIDE A BICYCLE

You may not always be able to use your two-wheeler—that 10-mile commute to work is a bit much—but riding a bike for short trips is a healthy alternative to driving for you and the environment. It saves gas (and gas money), creates zero pollution, reduces traffic congestion, and burns calories. Plus, you don't have to deal with the headaches associated with rush-hour traffic and finding a parking spot. According to the Department of Transportation, 40 percent of all car trips in the United States are two miles or shorter, and more than 25 percent are less than a mile—a distance that a bicyclist easily can cover in less than five minutes. So the next time you need to head down the street to pick up milk and bread, leave the car in the garage, grab a backpack, and hop on your bike.

An active biker is less likely to get heart disease or diabetes—and more likely to keep off unwanted pounds.

234 FUEL UP WITH FAT

If you're in the market for a new car, consider one that runs on biodiesel, a clean-burning fuel derived from renewable resources such as vegetable oils and animal fats. If you have a diesel car, you can switch to biodiesel with few or no modifications to your vehicle's engine or fuel system. Biodiesel contains no petroleum, but it can be blended with petroleum diesel at any percentage to create a blend. (For example, B20 is a blend of 20 percent biodiesel with 80 percent petroleum diesel.) Pure biodiesel emits more than 75 percent less carbon dioxide than petroleum diesel, and using a B20 blend reduces CO_2 emissions by 15 percent, according to the Department of Energy.

Biodiesel reduces our dependence on foreign oil because it's produced from plants grown on American soil—plants that absorb CO_2 while they're growing. However, biodiesel isn't a perfect solution. It may increase exhaust emissions of smog-causing nitrogen oxides, and critics point out that lots of land, water, and energy are needed to produce this alternative fuel. Research is ongoing to better serve U.S. fuel needs, of course. A recent development is using fast-growing algae, which has high oil content, as a source for biodiesel production. This would take pressure off of land-intensive crops such as soy and would generate many more gallons of biodiesel per acre than food crops.

Biodiesel is the only alternative fuel to have completed the health-effects testing requirements of the Clean Air Act. It is registered as a fuel with the Environmental Protection Agency and has been designated as an alternative fuel by the Department of Energy and the Department of Transportation. For a list of biodiesel retail locations, visit biodiesel.org.

235 TRY THE TELECONFERENCE

Do you travel for business? A handshake and a face-to-face meeting are sometimes a must—but not always. By making contact with colleagues and clients over the phone or online, you'll reduce fuel consumption and greenhouse gas emissions. You'll receive economic and time benefits, too. (Say goodbye to hotel rooms and flight delays!) Instead of relying on a carbon-emitting plane, train, or car, use the phone to conduct a meeting or the Internet to give a presentation. Technology keeps improving, making it easier to, say, be part of a Webinar, or Web seminar, in which material is presented to a large audience using the Internet. Advanced conferencing technology available at Web sites such as webex.com and gotomeeting.com allows participants to share applications, edit documents, demonstrate products, and provide training in real time. Teleconferencing is a globally friendly approach to working in a global business environment.

Companies that use teleconferencing can cut travel costs by around 30 percent per year.

236 FUEL-WISE WARM-UPS

The best way to warm up a vehicle is to drive it. Even on the bitterest of winter days, you don't need more than 30 seconds of idling before you're ready to hit the road. Idling for any longer wastes fuel. Idling for 10 minutes uses about 0.2 gallon of fuel—as much as it takes to travel five miles—and each gallon you use produces close to 20 pounds of carbon dioxide. Besides, idling only warms the engine, not the other parts (catalytic converter, transmission, and so on) that need to be warmed up, and the only way to warm these parts is to drive.

237 CARRY YOUR CLUBS

When Tiger Woods announced in August 2007 that he was designing a golf course in North Carolina, he said he'd "strongly encourage" golfers to walk the course. Dare we argue with the world's greatest golfer? Nope. Golf carts require gas or electricity. Gas-powered carts increase our dependence on oil and create pollution. Electric carts require energy to operate and charge. (It takes hours to fully recharge a cart.) Walking, which is good for your health and the course's health, minimizes your carbon footprint. It minimizes the dent in your wallet, too, because you won't have any cart fees. Next time you're at the course, drive the ball off the tee, but don't drive a cart. Carry or pull your clubs. Use the ambulating time to enjoy the scenery, chat with playing partners, or think about your next shot, which in all likelihood won't be as pretty as one of Tiger's.

Millions of people golf in the United States, and about half of them use a cart.

238 CHANGE YOUR IDLE WAYS

Idleness isn't an admirable trait in a person. It's not good when it comes to your car, either. An idling car is using gas to go nowhere. Getting 0 mpg isn't exactly efficient. Some sources suggest turning off the car every time you're waiting for more than 10 seconds. This isn't very feasible, so the recommendation here is to not let your car idle for more than 30 seconds when you're picking up a child at school or waiting for your spouse to cash a check—doing so burns more fuel than turning off the engine and restarting it. Some people argue that this practice shortens the life of the battery and starter, but the fuel savings—and the cleaner air—outweigh the minimal wear to these parts.

239 TAKE TRAINS, NOT PLANES

When it comes to trains versus planes, trains have their drawbacks. Travel times are longer. Tickets may be more expensive. Infrastructure may not make it possible to get anywhere near your destination city. But train travel has its advantages, too. Air-travel hassles are eliminated. (No waiting in long lines, taking off your shoes at the gate, visiting the baggage carousel, and so forth.) Passengers aren't as cramped, which makes it easier to take a nap or read the newspaper or work on that PowerPoint presentation. It offers a great way to see more of the country. And on the green front, it generates less pollution. It's impossible to say how much less because it depends on so many factors (distance, speed, number of passengers, age of the vehicle, and so on), but trains produce about two to three times less CO_2 per person per mile than planes generate. So unless you must take that cross-country flight to get to your meeting on time, consider "riding the rails" next time you travel. The environmental benefits make it worth the trip.

According to some estimates, emitting CO_2 into the upper atmosphere—which planes do—does more than twice the damage of the same amount of CO_2 emitted at ground level.

In addition to reducing pollution and saving energy, using mass transit eases road congestion; provides an opportunity to nap, read, work, or socialize; and offers a chance to exercise a bit because it usually involves walking to and from bus stops and subway stations.

240 USE MASS TRANSIT

Americans love their cars. In fact, close to 90 percent of all trips in the United States are made by car. And cars, as we all know, are the largest contributors to smog. Take a stand against air pollution by sitting down—on a bus or subway seat. If you have access to good public transportation, use it. Take it to get to work, to go to school, to go to the doctor, to sightsee on vacation. According to the American Public Transportation Association, public transportation in the United States saves 1.4 billion gallons of gas and reduces CO_2 emissions by more than 7.4 million tons each year.

Mass transit may not always be as convenient or enjoyable as taking the car, but you'll be doing something good for the planet by reducing our reliance on oil and cleaning our air. Hop on a bus—or subway or trolley or cable car or elevated train or ferry—today.

241 PERFORM ROUTINE MAINTENANCE

If you get regular tune-ups and perform routine maintenance on your automobile, you'll reduce emissions—which contributes to air pollution—and reduce our nation's dependence on foreign oil. The Environmental Protection Agency states that fixing a serious maintenance problem, such as a faulty oxygen sensor, can improve gas mileage by as much as 40 percent. An act as simple as replacing a dirty air filter can improve fuel economy by up to 10 percent.

Other ways to get better gas mileage include replacing worn spark plugs, making sure alignment is correct, fixing bad brakes, and using the grade of motor oil recommended by the car's manufacturer. (According to the Department of Energy, using a different motor oil can lower gas mileage by 1 to 2 percent.) Let the experts do what they can to make your engine purr like a kitten. Do what you can—everything from looking for loose wires or hoses to checking fluid levels—between tune-ups to keep it operating efficiently.

According to the Department of Energy, you can assume that for each 5 mph you drive over 60 mph your fuel economy drops 5 percent.

242 START DRIVING SMARTER

You don't have to have the most fuel-efficient car in the neighborhood. Just follow these four tips and you'll get more miles to the gallon.

- **Maintain a steady speed.**
- **Don't speed.** According to fueleconomy.gov, gas mileage usually decreases rapidly at speeds above 60 mph.
- **Avoid quick starts** and hard stops.
- **Don't weave** in and out of traffic.

With gas prices skyrocketing, aren't these driving habits worth considering?

243 CONSIDER AN ELECTRIC CAR

A battery electric vehicle, or BEV, which gets its power from energy stored in rechargeable battery packs, produces no exhaust fumes and reduces the country's dependence on petroleum. However, high costs, limited driving range between battery recharging, and lengthy charging times have prevented BEVs from being widely available. Until prices go down and performances (primarily through advances in battery technology) go up, BEVs will appeal more to the likes of George Clooney and Matt Damon than they do to the Average Joe.

Major car companies such as GM, Toyota, and Mitsubishi plan to launch electric vehicles for commercial sale within the next few years.

244 HIGH HOPES FOR HYDROGEN

If you want to move away from a gas-powered vehicle *and* be the first on your block to try something a bit extreme—and expensive—drive a car in which hydrogen is converted electrochemically in fuel cells to generate power. Hydrogen-powered fuel-cell cars use no petroleum and emit no CO_2, only oxygen and water vapor. Fuel cells aren't cheap though, and more research—on everything from fuel-cell technology to startup capability in cold weather—has to be done before hydrogen can become a viable alternative to fossil fuels. The federal government has already invested billions of dollars in research and development, and automakers are busy testing hydrogen cars, such as the Honda FCX, the Ford Focus FCV, and the General Motors HydroGen3. The main challenge, however, is developing infrastructure. It will be costly and complicated to get millions of fuel-cell cars on the road and create enough hydrogen filling stations. (There are less than 50 refueling stations in the United States, and most are in California.) It's a process that could take decades if hydrogen turns out to be the answer.

*"The civilized man has built a coach,
but has lost the use of his feet."*
— Ralph Waldo Emerson

245 WALK MORE OFTEN

A journey of a thousand miles begins with a single step. Confucius taught us that. A green journey begins with a single step, too. Just put one foot in front of the other and walk. Walk your children to school instead of putting them on the bus. Walk to the corner market for milk and bread instead of hopping in the car. Walk for a half hour after dinner instead of turning on the boob tube. We're all well aware that walking promotes better health (reduced risk of heart disease, improved coronary circulation, and so forth), but that's just the half of it. If you walk—the most environmentally friendly mode of transportation possible—you won't leave any footprints behind. Any carbon footprints, that is. So grab your iPod and start walking!

246 DON'T DRIVE NEEDLESSLY

Today's to-do list is a lengthy one. You need to get milk. You have to pick up clothes at the dry cleaner. You must make a deposit at the bank. You want to bring some soup to a sick friend. You need to return a book to the library. To be as earth-friendly as you can be, combine as many of your errands as possible into one trip. (Keep an errands list on the fridge to help you remember what needs to be taken care of when you leave the house.) A well-planned multipurpose trip is much more fuel efficient than making several short trips, each from a cold start. Making several short trips can use twice as much fuel as one multipurpose trip. You'll travel a shorter distance overall, which will save gas and diminish wear and tear on your vehicle.

247 CHOOSE A HIGH-MPG AUTO

So, you're in the market for a new car but just aren't quite ready to purchase a hybrid. That's OK, as long as you don't drive around town in a Hummer H3 or anything else that guzzles gas like there's no tomorrow. As manufacturers continue to fine-tune conventional engines, it's possible to find a car that gets a few extra miles per gallon. And more MPG means you'll pay less for gas and the earth will pay less for the negative aspects of its use. Do some research to find the most fuel-efficient standard vehicle you can afford. (Be sure to read those big stickers on the windows of new cars; they list Environmental Protection Agency MPG estimates.) At fueleconomy.gov, a Web site maintained by the Department of Energy and the EPA, you can do an MPG search by model year and class. You're not going to find a nonhybrid car that gets the gas mileage of a Toyota Prius, but you can find something with an overall MPG of around 30. Some models that may be worth looking into are Toyota Yaris, Honda Fit, Mini Cooper, Kia Rio, and Ford Focus. And, for goodness sake, stay away from that Lamborghini Murcielago, will you? It's gets less than 10 MPG in the city!

In an effort to encourage energy conservation," Orange, Connecticut, is allowing residents to file yearly requests for a full tax exemption on vehicles that have a federal rating of at least 40 MPG in city driving.

248 BE CENTRALLY LOCATED

Choosing where you live will have a huge impact on how much driving you'll do and how much fuel you'll consume. When you're thinking about moving, plot the houses you're considering on a map. How close are they to schools—and are they on school bus routes? And what about shopping centers, places of worship, and the public library? The difference of a few miles, over the course of years, can add up to hundreds of gallons of gasoline and many hours behind the wheel. Proximity to your place of work—or to major roads or public transportation that will take you there—is also an important factor in choosing a house. Check bus schedules and timetables. A community close to a commuter service is a plus when you resell, whether you commute or not.

CHAPTER 9

Green Building

*T*he greenest approach to building is nomadic. Mankind did it for thousands of years. Today, for better or worse, we've opted for four solid walls—and a lot more baggage. Nevertheless, there are ways to build that leave the environment less harmed.

CONTENTS

GENERATE WIND POWER

While wind power's biggest potential is with large-scale wind farms, a surprising number of small-scale wind turbines are purchased by homeowners. The best strategy is to combine wind power with photovoltaic (PV) solar energy. When winter winds give way to summer sun, the PV takes over. If you live in one of the many states that allow you to connect (intertie) with the utility company, your excess production can be fed into the electrical grid and credited to your account, or used as alternative energy boosters to, say, "turn your meter backward."

For wind power to work, you will probably need to have at least several acres of property and annual wind speeds averaging 8 or 9 mph. If your property is wooded, you will have to mount your turbine on a tower that is at least 30 feet above any obstruction within 500 feet, including buildings and trees. That's where the "clean" air is, meaning air that is undisturbed and hence more powerful.

The best way to determine whether you have enough wind to generate electricity is to measure it with a recording anemometer for a full year.

250 BUILD A SMALLER HOME

Before you build, ask yourself how much living space you really need. Every square foot costs between $5 and $10 per year to heat, cool, maintain, and pay taxes on.

Small houses are easier to heat and cool, use up fewer resources in their construction, and are easier to clean and maintain. If you're worried about not having enough space, universal design can make a small floor plan seem bigger. (See "Opt for Universal Design" on page 185.) Porches, decks, and patios also allow a house to expand when needed. Generations of Americans have grown up in homes well under 1,200 square feet. The average living space in Europe and Japan is 1,100 square feet.

251 SELECT CERTIFIED LUMBER

Be a conscientious consumer and seek out lumber sources that are certified by the Forest Stewardship Council (which operates worldwide) and the Sustainable Forestry Initiative (only in North America). These organizations regulate forestry operations to promote prompt reforestation, efficient wood utilization, and protection of water quality and wildlife habitats. Consumers can search for certified dealers at fscus.org and aboutsfi.org.

252 BUY THE RIGHT AMOUNT

Recycling and reusing construction materials are good strategies for lessening the demand upon natural resources. But buying only what you need is even better because it reduces both demand and waste. Estimate your needs by taking careful measurements and reading the labels on packages and cans. It's better for the environment for unneeded paint, adhesives, flooring, and the like to remain on the shelves at the home center than in your basement.

253 FIND A GREEN CONTRACTOR

Green building is a relatively new movement—and contractors are notoriously slow to change the way they do things. So finding an environmentally conscious contractor or designer when you're ready to move forward on a remodeling or building project may not be so easy. Word of mouth is good, of course. Check with local green building suppliers for recommendations. If you can't find a contractor that way, check with the U.S. Green Building Council (USGBC). The USGBC is a nonprofit trade organization devoted to expanding sustainable building practices that runs an accreditation program through its Green Building Certification Institute. You can find accredited members at its Web site, usgbc.org, in its state-by-state membership directory.

254 THE EMBODIED ENERGY FACTOR

An eco-conscious way to look at building materials is in terms of the energy it took to make them, or their "embodied energy." When building or remodeling, choose materials with the lowest embodied energy that will still do the job. For example, wood studs have a much lower embodied energy than steel studs. Fiber-cement siding has a lower embodied energy than vinyl siding. Work with designers that understand the complexity involved in making the right choices. And consider "recurring embodied energy," or the energy involved in maintaining building materials over many years. In short, it makes little sense to choose a product solely based on the energy it takes to make it if you'll have to use a lot of products with high embodied energy to maintain it.

A wood roof (left) has a much lower embodied energy than a steel or tile one.

255 PAINT IT GREEN

Paint has long been a Trojan horse in the home. For many decades the hidden danger was lead. In more recent formulations, it's been volatile organic compounds (VOCs). These gases are released during and after painting (often for years) and can cause a vast array of health problems, including headaches, asthma, and cancer. New laws have significantly lowered the allowed VOC levels in paints and related products. But you don't have to settle for a low-VOC product. Several paint manufacturers, including some major brands, now offer very low-VOC and zero-VOC paints. They cost a bit more than low-VOC paints but are healthier for you and more likely to have been manufactured in an environmentally friendly way.

256 BUILD A GREENER DECK

Wood is probably the most environmentally sound choice for deck building—as long as you're not using an endangered old-growth product. Wood is biodegradable, produces few if any toxic byproducts, and many species are fast growing and therefore renewable.

If preserved with today's copper compounds, such as alkaline copper quaternary (ACQ type B and D) and copper Azole (CA-B), it will last for decades. It poses no known threat to humans—although it may affect marine life. Avoid using wood that has not been certified by the Forest Stewardship Council (worldwide) and the Sustainable Forestry Initiative (North America).

Some experts consider recycled plastic lumber (RPL) a green option, too, because it saves trees and makes good use of plastics that would otherwise end up in landfills. RPL includes some all-plastic lumber products as well as many composite products that combine plastics and wood fiber. If buying the former, look for products that recycle polyethylene. If buying the latter, check the percentage of recycled material and the type of plastic before you buy. Some composite products are rated as less environmentally preferable by the Healthy Building Network (healthybuilding.net). These products are not biodegradable and cannot be separated back into plastic and wood waste.

"You never change things by fight-ing the existing reality. To change something, build a new model that makes the existing model obsolete."
— Buckminster Fuller

Composite lumber, which was used for the decking and balustrade of this deck, is made with recycled plastics and waste-wood fiber, but it cannot be separated economically and is not recyclable.

257 RECLAIM WOOD FOR FLOORS

Older is better, at least when it comes to wood. Wood harvested decades ago was often heartwood from old-growth trees. It was more stable, insect resistant, and had fewer knots. Today, you can work with flooring manufacturers or local recyclers who reclaim wood. Typically, it has been salvaged from condemned buildings, old logging sites, and even river bottoms. Old fasteners are removed, and the recovered materials are milled for use as flooring.

Reclaimed wood flooring is surprisingly available and has quality and character that are hard to match.

258 DAYLIGHT SAVINGS TIME

The use of sunlight in the home, called daylighting, is a great source of free energy, but to take advantage of it you need both openings through which the sun can shine and ways to control it when you don't want it. Windows, skylights, patio doors, and sunrooms are the most common openings. When building or remodeling, plan their locations carefully. A north-facing skylight, for example, can bring much-needed light into a kitchen or family room. A south-facing skylight may allow too much light—and heat—into the room.

Some basic rules:

• **South-facing windows** and patio doors are best for daylighting. They allow the winter sun to shine deeply into the home's interior, contributing heat as well. The windows should be shaded by eaves or awnings in the summer to prevent excessive heat gain.

• **North-facing windows** and skylights are also beneficial, producing a more even light with little glare.

• **East- and west-facing windows** allow light in during the morning and evening, respectively. You can take advantage of it by designing your home so the areas you use predominantly in the morning, such as the bathroom, face east—and the spaces you use in the afternoon and evening, such as the family room, face west.

• **Incorporate blinds** to control daylight. Blinds work best because they can be used to vary the amount of light according to preference.

• **Place your desk** near a window to reduce your need for artificial light.

• **Position your shades** to reflect direct light to the ceiling, preventing glare while still making good use of the sunlight.

Roof windows are a great way to make use of daylight. Face them north to avoid excessive heat buildup.

259 DON'T CHOP; TRANSPLANT

Before you cut down a healthy tree that's in the wrong location on your building site, consider transplanting it. Fairly large trees can be successfully moved and, though costly, may be an alternative to cutting them into firewood. Keep in mind that cutting down and disposing of a tree can be costly, too.

Penn State University's College of Agricultural Sciences Cooperative Extension has put out a fact sheet called "Plant with Care" that includes information on when to plant and how to plant correctly. The fact sheet can be found online at cas.psu.edu.

Fiber-cement siding, not to be confused with fiberboard siding, has the look and feel of wood at less cost.

260 GREENER SIDING

Be skeptical when someone suggests that polyvinyl chloride (PVC) is a green building material. It's not. This is especially true for vinyl siding. In fact, during its life cycle, from manufacture to disposal, it's extremely toxic and difficult to recycle. Should a vinyl-sided house catch fire, the dioxin-loaded fumes pose serious health risks for everyone nearby.

Better choices from both an environmental and aesthetic point of view include fiber-cement boards (they're made of cement, sand, wood fiber, and clay), stucco, and wood that has been certified by the Forest Stewardship Council.

261 GROW YOUR NEXT ROOF

The greenest roof is just that: green. It is made by layering plants and a growing medium over a filter membrane, drainage layer, waterproof membrane, and a moderately shaped roof deck (7 in 12 or less). Green roofs reduce heating and cooling costs; protect the roof membrane from damaging ultraviolet rays; and moderate rain runoff, preventing the overburdening of sewer systems. The biggest concerns with green roofs are leakage, the difficulty of making repairs, and cost. Weight, of course, is another concern. Your house may need to be reinforced to support the load. If your house is not a candidate for a green roof, see "Eco-Friendly Roofing" on page 193 for other green options.

Green roofs contribute to insulation, block roof-damaging UV rays, and help control rainwater runoff.

262 INSTALL ZONE HEATING

The ability to keep unused areas of the home cool while warming the spaces you're using will conserve large amounts of energy. The best time to install zone heating is when you're building a new house and using a hydronic heating (water- or steam-based) system. It works especially well with radiant heat. You can easily create zones with electric heating, too, but keep in mind that such systems are inefficient in cold climates and costly to operate.

263 LOSE YOUR VAC

Your portable vac, that is. Most units are noisy, cumbersome, and only marginally effective. If yours isn't of the high-performance variety, it may also be reintroducing allergens into your home via the machine's exhaust vent. Central vacs offer more power, clean better, and last longer, and you only need to change the dirt receptacles two or three times a year, saving bags and cost. Because the motor is located in the basement or utility room, they are less noisy, too.

With a central vacuum, there's no need to lug around a heavy machine. Just plug the hose and attachments into the nearest wall outlet.

264 PAINT IT EVEN GREENER

Try natural paints the next time you redecorate. They are made from natural substances such as plant oils, minerals, beeswax, and milk. Natural paint options include:

• **Natural clay paints:** Made from naturally occurring clays, they can be applied to most surfaces, including masonry and drywall.

• **Plaster:** A traditional paint alternative made from natural clays, plaster can be tinted and troweled on to any surface that absorbs water. New drywall and previously painted surfaces typically require priming first.

• **Milk paints:** Used in Colonial times, milk paints are made from milk, lime, and natural pigments. Milk paint does not flow out, as do conventional paints, so your brush marks will remain visible and give the surface texture rather than a smooth finish. Milk paint can be used outdoors as well.

• **Whitewash:** Similar to milk paints but usually without the milk, whitewash is made with lime and water and can be tinted with natural pigments. It too can be used indoors or outdoors.

Easy to repair, the clay-painted surfaces shown here can be sealed for added protection.

265 MAINTAIN; DON'T DEMOLISH

Millions of serviceable decks and other structures exist that were built with CCA (chromate copper arsenate) pressure-treated wood during the last few decades. Although the Environmental Protection Agency has banned its sale for residential use, and safer alternatives are now available, the sensible thing to do is to maintain it—not to demolish it. There is very little likelihood that the offending ingredient, arsenic, will be released in a harmful way. If you're concerned about your existing deck, use a penetrating oil finish or paint to reduce or eliminate exposure to CCA. You will probably need to reapply the finish every year or two. If you must remove an old deck, wear a dust mask. Discard sawdust and old boards according to your local laws. And never burn it in fire pits, wood-fired cooking appliances, or fireplaces, because this is the surest way to become exposed to the arsenic.

The green thing to do is to maintain existing structures made with CCA-treated lumber—not to remove them.

266 COMPOSTING TOILETS

Conventional toilets use dozens of gallons of clean water every day, while composting toilets use none. In addition, the latter allow you to recover what is a surprisingly useful resource. Called human waste by some and humanure by others, it can be used as a fertilizer as long as it has been completely and properly composted. Even urine can be turned into an odor-free liquid fertilizer by some units.

Don't want to add another chore to you hectic life? Some composting toilets have large enough holding tanks so they don't have to be emptied for many years. Composting toilets are best suited for use in cabins, cottages, RVs, and boats, but they are suitable for homes, too, especially in drought-prone regions where water conservation is imperative.

Note: outhouses are not composting toilets. They make it difficult to recover humanure. Worse, urine, which contains most of the valuable plant nutrients, leaches into the surrounding soil and eventually the groundwater.

Citrus-oil solvents contain no petroleum distillates. They're made from a renewable resource that's a byproduct of juice production.

267 USE SAFER SOLVENTS

Water is the safest solvent. But when you require something tougher, consider a citrus-based solvent. Made from the pulp that's left over after squeezing citrus fruit for juices, it will clean paint brushes and spills when you're using an oil- or alkyd-based finish. Plant-based solvents are a less toxic and environmentally sound option, but they should be used with caution nonetheless. Avoid skin contact; use in a well-ventilated area; and dispose of with other hazardous waste if you've cleaned a petroleum-based finish.

Universal design allows for more versatile living spaces, including wide doorways for wheelchair accessibility, should it ever be needed, and one-level living that allow seniors to stay in their homes longer.

268 OPT FOR UNIVERSAL DESIGN

Universal design is a broad concept that can affect everything from everyday tasks, such as the ease of handling a fork, to how long we can live in our homes. With the population of the United States aging, it can have a big impact on the environment in regard to conservation of resources. With more people able to stay in their homes longer, living productive lives, there will be less of a need to build more retirement communities, hospitals, and nursing homes. When building or remodeling, be sure to employ universal design ideas. Here is a starter list:

• **Opt for one-level living:** Cluster places to sleep, eat, and use the bathroom on one floor.

• **Think small:** Instead of designing a space for every need, consider designing spaces that are flexible and able to serve several purposes.

• **Avoid barriers:** Whenever possible, design without stairs, and incorporate wide doorways and hallways.

• **Choose the most ergonomic solution:** Use levers rather than twist knobs on doorways, touch controls for appliances and lighting, grab bars, and nonslip surfaces.

• **Pay attention to lighting:** Light for safety, security, and the task at hand. Avoid situations where glare or shadow can cause an accident.

For more information, visit aarp.org.

269 USE SALVAGED MATERIALS

Today, more than ever, there are warehouses full of building materials that have been removed from buildings slated for remodeling or demolition. Whether you're in a position to donate or buy, make use of this environmentally friendly trend the next time you plan a building project. For donors, the incentive is that you'll know your old cabinets, appliances, windows, and the like are going to good use—not to mention the tax deduction you'll be able to take. For those who can use old materials, there's the satisfaction of saving money, lightening the load on landfills, and conserving resources. As a bonus, used materials are often of better quality than the same materials purchased new.

For more information on finding sources for salvaged building materials, check out thereusepeople.org and buildingreuse.org.

270 IMPROVE VENTILATION

Turning on the vent fan in your kitchen or bathroom may not seem like a particularly green thing to do, but it is. The same is true about having good ventilation in your attic and basement. That's because moisture buildup causes numerous house problems that would otherwise require expensive repairs—and lots of resources. Problems associated with inadequate ventilation include mold growth, radon gas buildup, peeling paint, rotting wood, insect infestation, and insulation and roof shingle failure. As an added bonus, the well-ventilated home is easier to keep cool in the summer.

For good ventilation, use ridge, soffit, and gable vents. Solar-powered roof vents (above) are also available.

271 HIGH-EFFICIENCY FURNACES

Furnaces are usually categorized by their fuel efficiency, or AFUE ratings. AFUE stands for Annual Fuel Utilization Efficiency and averages performance throughout the heating season and during all phases of furnace operation. It tells you how much of the heat produced by your furnace is made available to your living space. The higher the number, the more efficient the furnace. For example, an AFUE of 80 percent means that 80 percent of the heating fuel is being converted to heat for the home. In 1992, a federal minimum efficiency standard for residential furnaces took effect. It requires that newly sold furnaces must have a minimum AFUE of 78 percent. Prior to that, furnace efficiencies ranged from 60 to 78 percent.

Today, there are two basic classes of furnaces commonly being sold: high-efficiency models (sometimes referred to as power combustion furnaces) that have AFUE ratings in the 80 to 82 percent range and super- or ultra-high-efficiency models (sometimes called condensing furnaces) that have AFUE ratings above 90 percent.

272 RENEWABLE FLOORING

Flooring must look good, stand up to abuse, clean easily, and be comfortable to walk on. For it to be green, it should also be manufactured from renewable resources. Your best bets include the following:

• **Cork** wins top honors for renewability. (You don't have to kill the tree to harvest the outer layer used for floors.) It's also at the top of the list for comfort.

• **Bamboo,** a type of grass, grows with amazing speed and is quite hard.

• **Linoleum,** not to be confused with vinyl, is a colorful green flooring alternative. It's made from a mix of linseed oil, resins, cork powder, wood flour, ground limestone, pigments, and a jute backing.

• **Engineered wood** is the real thing but uses resources in a more efficient manner. Instead of laying down a thick board of solid wood, engineered products are built up from layers, like plywood. Only the top layer is made from slow-to-renew hardwood.

• **Natural fiber** floor coverings, including wool, silk, sisal, cotton, and linen, offer beauty, comfort, and yet another renewable flooring option.

Cork flooring is not only renewable. It is beautiful, durable, and very comfortable to walk on.

273 RESTORE A HOUSE

Saving a worthy house from the wrecking ball also saves an enormous amount of materials and resources. In lumber alone, preserving an average-size home saves 16,000 board feet. That's equivalent to a 1 x 12-inch board more than 3 miles long! Add in the 20,000 to 30,000 nails and thousands of feet of wiring and piping and you begin to get an idea of the savings. In addition, older houses are often in prime locations, have historical value, and are better sized for the future than the oversize homes built in the recent past.

Neglected and in disrepair (top), the owners of this restored 208-year-old Colonial home saved enormous resources, as well as a bit of architectural heritage, by choosing not to tear it down.

274 GO FOR PASSIVE SOLAR

Passive solar energy has a high-tech ring, but it's actually quite simple. Think of it as any structure that's designed to capture energy from the sun for use as heat and illumination. Virtually any home can include passive solar elements, but most passive solar homes are oriented to get the most from the sun, usually with lots of south-facing windows. They also include thermal mass (earth, masonry, water, and so forth) to store the sun's heat for when it's needed. Finally, there's likely to be plenty of insulation (often including earthen roofs and berming) to reduce the home's overall heating requirements. As simple as it is, a passive solar home must be carefully designed. If not, overheating, mold growth, and poor indoor air quality are just a few of the problems that can occur. Fortunately, there are many sources for passive solar home designs. Choose one with designs tailored to your region.

Passive solar home designs are quite varied. Two things they all have in common are a way to store the winter sun's heat during the day so it can be used at night without relying on moving air by mechanical means (in this case, a masonry wall) and lots of insulation.

275 MAKE SOLAR ELECTRICITY

Electricity generated from sunlight—called photovoltaics, or PV, for short—has been successfully used to power everything from calculators and road signs to irrigation and telecommunications systems.

Residential applications, which were once limited to powering off-the-grid homes and vacation cabins in rural places, are now making inroads in suburbia as well. Two big reasons are the electric utility deregulation of the late 1990s and government incentives. Deregulation has enabled homeowners to connect (inter-tie) their PV systems to the power grid and get credit for their daily production on their electric bills. Called "net metering," homeowners pay only for the net amount of electricity they use. When the sun is shining during low-usage periods, electric meters actually spin backward. In the evening, the meter reverses direction as the family uses lighting and appliances and draws power from the grid. In effect, the utilities bank the power that homeowners produce—without the need for expensive and inefficient batteries.

Although still considered an expensive way to power your home, many states offer incentives to homeowners who want to install PV systems. Typically, rebates are given based on the amount of electricity their systems can produce. Other incentives include low-rate loans, grants, and tax rebates. If you live in California or New York, for example, the state-granted savings can come to nearly half the cost of your system. To learn more about federal and state-by-state incentives, visit dsireusa.org.

As electricity rates climb, producing your own electricity becomes more attractive. Regardless of the economics, these systems reduce consumption of fossil fuel and make more sense than nuclear energy.

Butcher block is good looking, functional, and green. Use in combination with other materials if you prefer a more water-resistant surface near sinks and other wet areas.

276 GREENEST COUNTERTOPS

It's not always easy to choose the most environmentally friendly material for your remodeling projects. Kitchen countertops, as well as tops for bathroom vanities, are cases in point. Here is a quick review of your choices:

- **Concrete** isn't made with petroleum-consuming plastics or resins, but it is energy intensive to manufacture and ship.
- **Stainless steel** is often made with recycled metals and is 100 percent recyclable, but there is the adverse impact of mining for the iron, nickel, and chromium to consider.
- **Stone, such as granite,** is a natural material but must be quarried, cut, polished, and shipped, all of which require lots of energy.
- **Solid-surfacing materials** can include recycled materials, but they are also likely to have a high content of petrol-based resins.
- **Plastic laminates,** which are made up mostly of compressed paper, use up fewer resources than some of the other materials, but also include resins and need to be attached to a substrate with eco-unfriendly adhesives.
- **Wood,** perhaps your greenest alternative, will require more maintenance than most of the other choices. It is however, naturally bacteria resistant. It's also renewable, biodegradable, and doesn't require a lot of energy to produce. Only buy wood from Forest Stewardship Council-certified sources. Use mechanical fasteners to attach it to your base cabinets.

277 ECO-FRIENDLY ROOFING

Most homes are roofed with asphalt shingles. It's not hard to understand why. They are effective, relatively inexpensive, easy to install, look OK, and even contain some recycled materials. Unfortunately, they are not very green; they're made up largely of asphalt, a product that relies on petroleum, and they don't last long. In a hot-weather climate, a 20-year rated product is likely to last for only 15 years. That means they end up producing a lot of waste.

The next time you must reroof, consider these greener products:

• **Copper, aluminum, and steel:** These materials are somewhat more eco-friendly than asphalt because they last up to four times longer, have a lower shipping weight, and are easily recycled. But metals also have an adverse impact at the beginning of their life cycle, including mining issues, pollution, and large expenditures of energy.

• **Wood:** Natural and usually longer-lasting than asphalt, wood shingle roofs would seem to be green. Many experts, however, don't see the harvest of old-growth red cedar as sustainable. Cost and regular maintenance are other drawbacks.

• **Tile:** Made of concrete or clay, tile is a long-lasting roofing solution that makes use of plentiful, recyclable materials. Tile is heavy to ship, and tile roofs may require structural modifications for support.

• **Solar shingles:** Photovoltaic (PV) solar shingles or PV panels offer a long-lasting roof that will produce electricity for your home as well. The negative is high initial cost. And you'd still have to hire a contractor to install conventional roofing on the north-facing portions of your roof.

Tile roofing is a green choice because it lasts and because it's made from materials that are plentiful. Opt for nearby producers when possible.

278 SAVE A PRECIOUS TREE

Trees are beautiful, can reduce energy consumption, protect from strong winds, reduce erosion, filter air of pollutants, and enhance real-estate values. But too often homeowners and their

A mature tree's root system is mostly in the top 6 inches of soil and often extends beyond the tree's dripline (outermost leaves).

contractors give little thought to trees when planning home additions and other improvements. Excavating for foundations and swimming pools, for example, can damage trees dozens of yards away from the action.

To improve a tree's chances of survival, protect as much of it's root zone as possible during construction and landscaping projects. The rule of thumb, according to the International Society of Arborculture, is to fence off a root protection zone equal in radius to 1 foot for every inch of trunk diameter. Within this area, avoid trenching, rototilling, regrading, soil compaction, and storage of materials, such as topsoil and debris.

Prune tree canopies to permit passage of equipment. This will reduce the risk of unnecessary damage and help prevent tree disease later. Also, prune roots first, rather than tear them with excavation equipment, when you have no choice but to dig within the root zone.

When the surrounding grade around trees must be raised, use gravel-filled tree wells to maintain the existing root depth. Conversely, use retaining walls to preserve the original grade around trees when the surrounding grade must be lowered.

279 PUT HEAT UNDERFOOT

Radiant heat is considered the most desirable home-heating method because it heats people, not air. A properly designed system will not only be fuel-efficient but will be far more comfortable than conventional heating, too. Radiant heating systems typically consist of a network of tubing embedded in a concrete slab. The tubing may also be affixed to aluminum plates or placed under a gypsum underlayment. Warm water continuously circulates in the pipes, warming the floor. It is thermostatically controlled, like any heating system. Leak-prone copper tubing of earlier systems has been replaced by tough plastic tubing. Electric radiant heat is also available but is less efficient.

280 GREEN UP YOUR TOOLBOX

In the realm of tools, green is spelled h-a-n-d. For millennia, man built and fixed things without power tools. If you're the average homeowner who only needs to do occasional boring, sawing, and sanding, consider investing in a good egg-beater-style hand drill, a few quality handsaws, a plane, and a sanding block. If you're a bit more ambitious—you build shelves and install moldings, for example— buy used power tools from online listing services, such as craigslist.com.

There's no reason to add to the earth's load of millions of underused portable power tools. If you must have your own, invest in top-quality tools that will last decades. Don't buy cheap "homeowner-grade" tools from mass marketers. They won't last and give poor results. *Consumer Reports* provides valuable information on making quality tool selections.

For many jobs around the house, hand tools work just fine. In addition to the tools mentioned above, include an awl—for making starter holes for screws—in your tool kit.

281 SOLAR POOL HEATING

Solar collectors designed for pool water heating are an eco-friendly alternative to conventional gas-fueled pool heaters. Unlike solar collectors used for domestic hot water, they are typically unglazed and made from a specially formulated plastic.

They're also uncomplicated to operate and easy to maintain. Water from the pool is circulated through the solar collectors using the existing water filtration pump. At night, or when the weather is cloudy, a diverting valve closes off the collector circuit. Costs range between $2,000 and $10,000. Payback periods range from 18 months to 7 years.

However you heat your pool water, use a pool cover to prevent heat loss at night or on cool days.

282 DON'T SKIMP ON THE FRIDGE

A refrigerator is the largest appliance you'll put in your kitchen. It eats up the most energy, too, accounting for up to 15 percent of a household's energy consumption. Save some energy by investing in an efficient fridge. The most efficient models on the market today use about 400 kWh per year, which is up to four times less energy than they used 35 years ago. And those with the Energy Star label use at least 15 percent less energy than required by federal stan-

dards. According to the Department of Energy, top-mount refrigerators (those with freezers on the top) use less energy than bottom-mount or side-by-side models.

Whichever configuration you choose, don't get one that's too big—or small—for your needs. An average family of four needs 20 to 22 cubic feet of storage space, but if you have a couple of teenagers who are food vacuums, consuming milk and sandwiches like there's no tomorrow, you may want a larger unit.

283 LOOK FOR THE ENERGY STAR

Want to help protect the environment? Look for products with the blue Energy Star label, which is on major appliances, heating and cooling equipment, home electronics, and office equipment. These products have met strict energy-efficiency guidelines set by the Environmental Protection Agency and the Department of Energy. Using Energy Star refrigerators, washing machines, programmable thermostats, ceiling fans, televisions, computers, and other products saved Americans $14 billion on their utility bills in 2006 and reduced greenhouse gas emissions equivalent to those from 25 million cars. The typical household spends close to $2,000 a year on energy bills. With Energy Star products, which use 10 to 50 percent less energy than standard models, you can save up to 30 percent, or $600, annually—and save on greenhouse gas emissions. For more information, including tools and resources to help plan projects to reduce your energy bills, visit energystar.gov.

Energy Star refrigerators use at least 15 percent less energy than required by federal standards; Energy Star washing machines use 50 percent less energy than standard washers and can save more than 20 gallons of water per load.

284 THINK OUTSIDE THE BOX

Cabinets put significant demands on the environment. The fronts are made from ever-scarcer hardwoods. Petroleum is used for wood finishes and adhesives. Energy is needed to forge the hardware.

There are less expensive—and more ecological—ways to keep your kitchen well ordered. Open shelves, for example, make access and visibility easier—and use up far less wood. Wall and ceiling racks are great ways to store frequently used cookware, reducing the need for cabinets. Drawer organizers and dividers improve storage efficiency, too.

If your heart is set on the traditional cabinet, buy a quality line. In general, the more solid wood or high-grade plywood, the better. High-density polymers and medium-density fiberboard (MDF) can also produce a good cabinet. Avoid cabinets with face frames (rails and styles), shelving, backs, or drawers made with particleboard.

285 INSULATE THE GARAGE

Garage doors are typically the largest opening in a home. In winter, they contribute to heat loss, especially if the door to the house is not insulated, or if the garage is heated. Similarly, they contribute to heat gain in summer. When replacing old doors or building a new garage, choose doors with foam-in-place polyurethane cores and an R-value of at least 11. The R-value of polyurethane is twice as high as polystyrene insulation. Look for a flexible bottom door seal to stop infiltration on the doors you purchase as well.

286 BUY GREENER DOORS

Don't lose energy, not to mention comfort, because you've purchased an exterior door that has poor insulation and isn't well sealed. An energy-efficient door will keep your indoor air in and the outdoor air out. Steel and fiberglass doors with a polyurethane foam core are the most energy efficient. They insulate better than wood doors, which have a traditional look but are susceptible to the elements.

Doors with the Energy Star label have tighter fits and improved weather stripping, and their frames may include a magnetic strip—similar to those found on a well-constructed refrigerator—to create a tighter seal that reduces drafts around the edges.

Take U-factor into account, too. U-factor is a measure of the rate of heat transfer; the lower the U-factor, the better the door insulates. (Values generally range from 0.25 to 1.25.) Solid doors are more energy efficient than doors with windows, but if you are getting a door with a glass panel, look for double panes, which offer better insulation than single panes.

And remember: a door is only as good as its installation.

287 ERECT A PERGOLA

A great way to cool your house in the summer—and beautify your patio—is with a pergola. Similar to arbors, pergolas are built adjacent to the house. A trellis-like roof allows you to grow vines, such as grape or wisteria, which will help shade walls, windows, and patio doors. They're a cool place to sit in the summer, too.

288 HEAT WATER WITH THE SUN

Heating your domestic hot water with the sun is a time-tested technology that would save the United States millions of barrels of oil every year—and save you 20 to 40 percent of your energy costs. Today's solar hot-water systems are vastly improved over their predecessors, with better collectors and more sophisticated controls. There are more qualified installers than ever before, too. Some states offer financial incentives, but if you have a good site, the payback period is reasonable even without them—only three to five years in most regions across the United States.

289 BUILD A SOLAR SHOWER

Save energy—and treat yourself to pure bliss while doing it—with an outdoor solar shower. Heat the water with a coil of black hose, a black-painted water tank, or with a large black plastic water bag, sold for the purpose. You'll only need to leave them in the sun for an hour or two. In addition to saving the fossil fuels that heat up your water heater, you can use the "gray" shower water to irrigate garden beds instead of sending it to the sewers. Just be sure to use biodegradable soaps, rinses, and shampoos. For more information, search "solar shower" on the Internet.

290 ENERGY-EFFICIENT WINDOWS

Two panes of glass, with an air- or gas-filled space in the middle, insulates much better than a single pane of glass and can help reduce your utility bill by up to 10 percent. You'll also want to mind your p's and q's—make that e's and u's. A low-e (low-emittance) coating reflects infrared light, limiting the amount of heat loss in the winter and heat gain in the summer. U-factor measures the heat transfer through a window; the lower the U-factor, the better the window insulates. The most energy-efficient window framing is fiberglass, wood, or vinyl. Aluminum, because it's a heat conductor, is a poorer choice. Well-insulated windows offer energy savings, of course, but they also provide noise reduction, which is nice when the neighbor has revved up his leaf blower.

The installation of energy-efficient windows may quality you for a tax break.

CHAPTER 10

Conserving Water

Water use and water pollution are inextricably bound—whether it's fertilizer-laden lawn runoff finding its way into lakes or medications being flushed into sewers. There are also areas where water is simply scarce. Here are some easy ways to use less.

CONTENTS

USE LOW-FLOW DEVICES

Installing aerators on your faucets can save thousands of gallons of water a year. Aerators mix air into the water stream, maintaining the pressure but using considerably less water. Install an aerator if your older faucet accepts it (check for threads inside the tip of the faucet), or replace the aerator on a newer faucet if its flow rate is too high. New kitchen faucets typically come with aerators that restrict flow rates to 2.2 gallons per minute (gpm) at 60 pounds per square inch (psi), while bathroom-faucet aerators restrict flow rates to from 1.5 to 0.5 gpm—compared with 3 to 6 gpm for older faucets.

Aerators are easy to install and inexpensive; they cost about $10 at home-improvement and hardware stores. Some come with shutoff valves that allow you to stop the flow of water without affecting the temperature, another water-saving feature.

Equipping a faucet with an aerator is a simple way to reduce water consumption by as much as 50 percent. Save even more by installing a low-flow showerhead, which restricts water flow without restricting pressure. Today's showerheads must not exceed 2.5 gpm at a water pressure of 80 psi.

292 MAKE MULCH YOUR FRIEND

Mulch takes many forms, from pine bark to plastic. Economy-minded gardeners recycle newspaper and even old carpeting for use as mulch. Whatever material you choose, mulch serves three important functions: it combats the growth of weeds, slows evaporation of water from soils, and prevents soil erosion. If you're using bark, pine needles, or wood chips, be sure to apply a thick layer of at least 5 inches to discourage weed growth.

For best results with mulched beds, use an underlayment of water-permeable landscape fabric. To prevent trunk rot, pull the mulch 6 inches away from the base of trees or shrubs.

293 UPGRADE YOUR CONTROLLER

Watering lawns and gardens accounts for 30 percent of the water used by the average homeowner. Much of that water—up to 24 billion gallons per year across the United States—is wasted. If you own an automatic irrigation system, consider upgrading to a weather-based, or ET (evapotranspiration) controller. These high-tech controllers let you schedule when each lawn zone will be watered and for how long, and they utilize data from nearby weather stations and/or from sensors that monitor site conditions to determine how fast water is being lost from the soil and from plants. Weather-based controllers use the data to calculate the most effective watering schedule for your lawn on any given day. You end up giving your lawn and landscape the water it needs—and no more.

If you water your lawn with portable sprinklers, invest in an inexpensive timer, which makes it impossible to waste water by forgetting to turn the sprinkler off.

294 DON'T WASH CLEAN CLOTHES

You wear something once and throw it in the washing machine because it must be dirty and smelly. But is it? Or can it be worn two or three more times before washing? Items such as jeans, skirts, and sweaters can usually be worn more than once. In fact, your clothes may last longer, as washing and drying wears out clothing. If you've spilled spaghetti sauce on your blouse or sweat profusely through your T-shirt while working in the garden, then by all means wash it. But if an article of clothing isn't really dirty (or smelly), don't wash it. You'll save water and energy. Most of the environmental impact associated with clothing comes not from its production or distribution but from laundering.

295 TAKE SHORTER SHOWERS

Simply wash and rinse a little quicker. Seems obvious. But it's not so easy, especially if you're a shower lover. One solution is to buy a handheld shower set with a shutoff button. That way you can turn off the water while you lather—and turn it back on easily without having to stop and readjust the water temperature. Handheld shower heads also allow you to rinse more efficiently. Other tips:

• **Do not shave in the shower**—unless you shut off the water first.

• **Set a timer** for five minutes and resolve to beat the clock.

• **Exercise in the morning,** before showering. You'll need less warm water and will be less likely to need a second shower later in the day.

Shorter showers will also save energy—and money.

Shut off the water while you lather. Each minute that the shower isn't running saves about 2 gallons of water.

296 INSTALL A GRAY-WATER SYSTEM

Gray water is wastewater from washing machines, bathtubs, showers, and bathroom sinks but *not* from kitchen sinks, dishwashers, or toilets. Recycling water generated when you do laundry or bathe—assuming the cleaning products you use don't contain harsh chemicals—is a great way to conserve our fresh water supplies.

Gray water, which is *not* clean enough to drink, can be used to flush toilets, water houseplants and ornamental gardens, and irrigate lawns. Using a bucket in the shower to catch water while you're waiting for it to heat up and attaching a hose to your washing machine's water outlet and piping it directly to a mulch basin are two simple ways to use gray water. (Don't, however, store untreated gray water for more than a day—it becomes anaerobic and starts to smell bad.) A more complex system may include underground pipes leading to a settling tank designed to filter and store the water before it's distributed via a pump.

Knowing how much water will be treated and what you'll be using it for will help you determine what type of system to install. If you're considering such a system, check with local authorities to see if formal approval is required.

297 USE WATER-SAVING TOILETS

In the average home, the toilet accounts for more than 25 percent of water use. You can use less of this valuable resource if you consider a low-flush, dual-flush, or composting toilet.

Low-flush toilets, which are mandated by plumbing codes, are required to use 1.6 gallons or less per flush, which is about half the water older models use. And today's low-flush models are better than the first ones that came along, so you don't have to flush multiple times to get the job done, which negated any water savings. A two-buttoned or two-handled dual-flush toilet, which is common in Europe, allows you to control the flushing—a small flush for liquid waste and a bigger flush for solid waste. For example, the Aquia Dual Flush Toilet by Toto provides 0.9 gallon for liquids and 1.6 gallons for solids. A composting toilet, which converts human waste into organic compost through aerobic decomposition, uses little or no water.

"*We never know the worth of water till the well is dry.*"
— *Thomas Fuller*

Toilets in the average home get flushed about five times each day. Replacing an older toilet with a low-flow model can prevent you from flushing water—and money—down the drain.

298 CHECK SPRINKLER COVERAGE

If you water with an automated in-ground sprinkling system, make sure it's delivering even coverage. To check for even coverage, place several shallow containers around the area being watered. Tuna fish cans work well. Check the cans after 30 minutes. If one container has less water than the others, you may have a problem with the sprinkler head nozzle, spacing of sprinkler heads, or system pressure at outlying sprinkler heads. Unequal water distribution from sprinklers typically results in excessive run times to soak the "dry" spot—and significant amounts of wasted water.

It's important to adjust sprinkler systems, such as the spray-type heads seen here, so they don't overspray water onto walls, walks, driveways, and streets.

299 SAVE TOILET WATER

Buying a better toilet isn't the only way to save water. (See "Use Water-Saving Toilets" on page 206.) Try these tips and you're likely to save water without having to shell out for a new toilet.

• **Checks for leaks.** Even a moderate leak could waste hundreds of gallons of water a day. To test for leaks, simply add a few drops of food coloring to the tank and wait 10 to 15 minutes. If color appears in the bowl, you have a leak.

•**Avoid unnecessary flushing.** Don't use the toilet as a trash can, flushing tissues, bugs, pills, and dead goldfish. And don't always feel the need to flush after urinating. Remember: "If it's yellow, let it mellow. If it's brown, flush it down."

• **If you've got an older toilet,** fill a 2-liter bottle with sand or pebbles and put it in the tank. It will act as a water-displacement device and reduce the water lost per flush. Don't use a brick as a water-displacement device in your tank—it will slowly decay and may cause plumbing problems that will eventually lead to a new toilet anyway.

300 TURN OFF THE TAP

Doing a basic home experiment proves that leaving the faucet running while brushing your teeth for 60 seconds uses 6 to 14 cups of water, depending on the water pressure. Assuming you do what the dentist says and brush those pearly whites twice a day, every day, you're wasting approximately 275 to 650 gallons of water a year. Instead, turn the faucet on just long enough to fill a small cup (for rinsing) and to soften the brush's bristles. (Stiff bristles can damage your gums.) Turn it off. Brush. Turn it on again for a few seconds to rinse the brush. (Rinsing removes toothpaste residue and debris.)

The same water-saving methods apply to rinsing a shaving razor—filling a cup with water is better than letting gallons go down the drain.

According to the American Dental Association, you should brush your teeth twice a day for several minutes each time, but that doesn't mean you have to let the water run constantly.

301 TRY A WATERLESS CAR WASH

If you wash your car at home for only 10 minutes, you could be wasting more than 100 gallons of water. Instead, try a waterless car wash for a vehicle that isn't excessively soiled or muddy. These non-toxic formulas are simply sprayed onto a car's exterior, where they absorb and dissolve dirt and grime, and then wiped off with microfiber towels. The best part is that wax is a part of the formula, so no separate waxing is necessary. Look for a product that is free of kerosene and silicone. (Check out freedomwaterlesscarwash.com for more information.)

Mounting your rain barrel on a wall eliminates any need for siphoning. For rainwater that is as clean as possible, keep your roof free of debris and do not apply any toxic chemicals to the roof.

302 COLLECT RAINWATER

During a moderate rainfall, your roof will likely shed more than 100 gallons of water. By catching it in a barrel, it can be put to use irrigating plants during dry periods. All you need is a barrel (50 to 75 gallons should suffice) with a fine screen on top and a faucet at the bottom. The screen catches leaves (and other debris) and keeps out mosquitoes, birds, pets, and children. You can purchase a barrel or make your own relatively easily. Instructions can be found on many Web sites. (For more information, visit rainbarrelguide.com.)

As an added bonus, rainwater improves the health of trees, plants, flowers, and lawns because it doesn't contain magnesium, chlorine, and other chemicals. Attach a hose to the barrel's faucet and you can use the water to wash windows or the car. If you have a well and your water pump fails, you'll have water you can use to flush the toilet. Do *not* use the water for drinking or cooking. If you're interested in doing so, you'll have to install a filtering system.

303 FIND AN ECO CAR WASH

If the family vehicle is so dirty you fear an inconsiderate stranger is going to finger "WASH ME" on your hood yet you aren't up for doing a waterless wash at home (see the opposite page), visit a professional car wash that will provide a green clean. You'll save water because while a home wash typically uses more than 100 gallons, a pro car wash uses less than 45 gallons per car, on average. Pro car washes treat dirty water before it's disposed, but find out if the company recycles its water. Also ask if it captures and utilizes rainwa-ter. Inquire about other environmentally friendly measures it takes, too, such as the use of solar panels on the roof or the use of energy-efficient equipment and lighting. To protect the planet *and* your car's exterior, choose an establishment that uses nontoxic, biodegradable soaps and natural waxes.

Professional car washes treat waste water so that toxic chemicals (from cleaning detergents, gas, oil, and so forth) don't get into our rivers and oceans.

304 A PITCH FOR PITCHERS

How often do you stand at the faucet, with a drinking glass in hand, running the tap and waiting for the water to get cold? That's a lot of water going down the drain, which isn't exactly the most earth-friendly way to go about quenching your thirst. Keep a pitcher—one that filters, if you prefer—filled with water in the refrigerator and cold water will be available whenever you want it. Reward yourself by adding mint leaves or slices of lemon, lime, or cucumber to the pitcher. You'll save gallons of water each month while lowering your water bill at the same time—something we can all drink to.

305 WHEN TO WASH BY HAND

Contrary to what many believe, using the dishwasher uses less water than washing by hand, even for the most conscientious hand washers. A dishwasher uses just 4 to 6 gallons per cycle, and washing by hand can use 10 to 20 gallons. Having said that, when you have only a few lightly soiled items, do them by hand. You'll save energy over time by reducing the number of times you have to run the dishwasher. (Dishwashers use about 300 to 600 kWh/year.) Wash wisely, though. Don't keep the hot water running. Fill up the sink or a bucket, and soak the items in soapy water.

306 REDUCE LAWN WATERING

The biggest use of water by many homeowners is lawn irrigation. With costs rising and water-use restrictions in many municipalities, here are some ways to conserve:

• **Water early in the morning.** Less water will be lost to evaporation.

• **Keep your grass relatively tall.** The plants will then help reduce evaporation by shading the soil.

• **Plant native or drought-resistant grasses** when reseeding. They will need less watering because they are better adapted to your climate.

• **Work to improve your soil by top-dressing** with organic material and by leaving your grass clippings where they fall after mowing. Organic material acts as a kind of mulch and holds water longer in the soil.

• **Aerate your soil** with a core cultivator. Aeration promotes deeper root growth. When combined with infrequent, deep waterings, it enables grass plants to take moisture from a greater soil area.

• **Keep chemicals off your lawn.** Organic lawns require less watering than chemically treated ones.

• **Use a sharp mower blade** for cleaner cuts. Cleanly cut lawns look greener and lose less moisture to evaporation.

• **Do not overfertilize.** Unnecessary growth uses water unnecessarily.

• **Direct downspouts** and other sources of runoff to your lawn, not to the driveway or street.

• **Allow your lawn to temporarily brown-out** or go dormant when drought conditions persist. This will not hurt a healthy lawn.

307 BUY WATER-EFFICIENT WASHERS

When buying a washing machine, your biggest decision is top-loading or front-loading. If you don't mind spending a bit more money up front, go with the latter. Using a front-loader can save about 15 to 20 gallons per wash, cutting water use by about half—the equivalent of 13,000 gallons per year! They save energy and are gentler on clothes, too. Plus, their high-speed spin cycle extracts more water, which cuts down on drying time. While we're on the subject of dryers, choose one that runs on gas and you'll contribute 60 percent less CO_2 to the air than if you used an electric model. Better yet, use the sun.

308 DRIP; DON'T SPRAY

Drip irrigation puts water where you need it—at the base or roots of a plant—using a network of plastic tubing, emitters, and small spray nozzles. Unlike portable and in-ground sprinklers, very little water is wasted due to evaporation or spraying water where you don't need it, such as house walls and driveways.

Drip irrigation is particularly well suited to watering trees and shrubs but can also be used for vegetable and flower gardens, lawns, and potted plants. Systems can be set up with controllers or timers and can also be used to deliver fertilizer while you irrigate. Finally, drip-irrigation systems tend to be easier to maintain than in-ground systems.

Drip-irrigation systems are not only efficient, they're unobtrusive and quiet, too. Tubing can be covered by mulch, as shown.

CHAPTER 11

Spreading the Word

Anyone who was around during the 1970s knows that energy conservation and alternative energy were hot topics. Over the next few decades, however, momentum fizzled. But not all was lost. The green spirit was passed along to a new generation that has embraced it like no other. Let's be sure to continue to spread the word.

CONTENTS

SHARE WHAT YOU KNOW

The best way to teach a child about the environment? Get outside. Protecting the environment isn't an abstract concept, after all. If our society seems blind to our natural world, it might be because we see so little of it. Take a hike and make a game of identifying trees, insects, and flowers.

Paddle a canoe, swim in a nearby lake, camp in a state park. At home, planting a garden or a tree, or identifying a rock, can make the environment come alive for a child. And child or not, watching a tomato appear for the first time is wondrous.

When you're back inside, talk to your child about why you recycle or make compost. There are many green Web sites for younger and older children. View the Environmental Protection Agency's kid-friendly Web sites (epa.gov/kids and epa.gov/students) with your children. The National Resources Defense Council has a clever Web site for kids, too (nrdc.org/makewaves).

The best way to ensure a greener future is to get children on board now. Besides, they can be very good at reminding you to practice what you preach!

310 TAKE AN ACTIVE INTEREST

What environmental issues are you concerned about? Climate change? Energy consumption? Deforestation? Fair trade? Show your support of, or opposition to, an issue. That's being an activist. You can be an activist without being, well, all that active. Without getting up, you can contact a senator or representative. You can sign an online petition. You can take part in a sit-in and blog about it while it's happening. If you don't mind getting up, you can hand out flyers, lobby at city hall, or stage a fundraiser.

Don't be a spectator. Be a participator. You're not alone; like-minded people and groups are out there. If you'd like help getting started, the Web sites for the National Resources Defense Council (nrdc.org) and the Sierra Club (sierra-club.org) have an "Action Center." Other sites you might want to check out include care2.com and idealist.org.

311 SUPPORT OPEN SPACES

Green spaces are valuable. Parks, forests, wetlands, and the like provide habitats for wildlife, give children a place to play, reduce air pollution, and increase area property values. Acres and acres of open spaces are disappearing by the hour. It's important to stand up and be counted when natural areas are in danger of becoming homes, roads, and shopping centers. Support open space initiatives on the local ballot. Donate to organizations that are protecting land—a finite resource—from overdevelopment. Greet any chance to preserve open space with open arms.

312 CELEBRATE EARTH DAY

Find a local Earth Day event and celebrate the holiday that helped found the modern environmental movement. Created by U.S. Senator Gaylord Nelson in 1970, the first Earth Day rallies captured the growing concern that Americans felt about their damaged environment. Shortly after the 1970 rallies, Congress created the Environmental Protection Agency and passed the Clean Air Act. Earth Day has gone global: 175 countries mark it every April 22. See earthday.net for additional information.

No time for Earth Day? How about Earth Hour, where cities around the world turn off lights for one hour? Check it out at earthhour.org.

"We are on a spaceship; a beautiful one. It took billions of years to develop. We're not going to get another. Now, how do we make this spaceship work?"
— *Buckminster Fuller*

313 ENVIRONMENTAL ORGANIZATIONS

Our world would be in far worse shape if not for eco-watchdog organizations. In the political arena, nonprofits such as the Sierra Club and the National Resources Defense Council have watched over the Environmental Protection Agency, making sure that environmental statutes such as the Clean Air Act are enforced. In the areas of conservation and biodiversity, groups such as the World Wildlife Fund and the Nature Conservancy have secured land for generations still unborn and pre-served critical habitats for threatened species. The Ocean Conservancy and the Blue Ocean Institute have taken the public beneath the surface of the waves, showing us, tragically, how empty our seas now are. These and other important organizations rely on contributions for survival. They may receive major grants from foundations, but small donations from people across the country are what give them power.

314 SUBSCRIBE TO A GREEN 'ZINE

It may be small comfort, but environ-mentally speaking we're better informed than ever before. Support quality journalism by subscribing to an environmental magazine. The new *Plenty* is hip and lively. *Orion* is the intel-lectual's eco-journal, with contributions from many top writers. *E: The Environmental Magazine* is a nuts-and-bolts bible. *Audubon* is a must-read for anyone interested in conservation.

315 PLANT A TREE ON ARBOR DAY

Founded in the late nineteenth century by a Nebraska newspaper editor who believed his state would never attract residents without trees—back then, Nebraska was a treeless plain—Arbor Day has exploded into a holiday that's honored by communities planting trees around the world. In the United States, each state celebrates Arbor Day on a different weekend in the spring, whenever tree planting is easiest. (The fall is another good time to plant a tree.) The remarkable Arbor Day Foundation, which gives trees to new members, has all the information you need to put in a tree this year. See arborday.org.

316 HELP WITH A CLEANUP

Picking up litter made the headlines in the 1960s when First Lady Lady Bird Johnson put her glamour behind the Keep America Beautiful (KAB) organization. Cleaning up communities has rarely been high-society since, but it remains every bit as important, and the KAB, now a half century old, is still spiffing up America's streets and playgrounds. Many cities depend on these and other community cleanup efforts; without individual initiatives, there would be a lot more trash blowing in our wind. Visit kab.org for more information about the Keep America Beautiful program, which relies on public-private partnerships and has more than 1,000 affiliates across the country. And contact your local and state government to see if there are any established community cleanups. If there aren't any, act. Many municipalities will happily loan groups trash bags and other supplies.

You won't have to look far for a site in need of cleaning. Be sure that all helpers are equipped with work gloves.

Your child will remember his or her first fishing trip forever. The experience will help form his ideas about conservation and the environment.

 **TAKE A CHILD FISHING**

A child who knows how to fish knows that all elements in an ecosystem are interconnected. To catch fish, you need to have a well-managed stock of them; to eat fish, you need to have clean water. Our oceans, lakes, and rivers are damaged partly because they look healthy from a distance. That's why fishing is important—it lets you look beneath the surface. A fishing spot that's been shut down is an argument for action.

318 BOOKMARK GREEN WEB SITES

It often seems as if environmentalists spend most of their time in the virtual world. The energy and diversity of the many, many green Web sites out there never fails to astonish. Here are our top three: for political coverage, see the smart, always entertaining grist.org. For environmental news with style, check out treehugger.com. And worldchanging.com has the lowdown on many new eco-initiatives worldwide.

319 GET STARTED IN SCOUTING

Enroll your child in a scouting program. The Boy Scouts and Girl Scouts organizations are both almost a century old and have long been focused on teaching children about nature and conservation. Their "learn by doing" approach takes environmental education out of the classroom and into the great outdoors. Whether it's learning how to tell the difference between a maple and an oak or developing a program to protect local watersheds, scouting has something to offer every child. Check out scouting.org and girlscouts.org. And if you do sign up your child, sign up yourself to help, too. It's a treat!

Protecting the environment is about more than ensuring our survival as a species. It's also about developing a keen appreciation for the outdoors—and for a perfectly roasted marshmallow.

320 VISIT A GREEN DESTINATION

If you're planning a trip, look into stopping by a green destination—there are more environmentally focused institutes, workshops, and festivals than ever. To entice you, here are a few of our favorites: California's Solar Living Institute hosts year-round workshops and an annual SolFest (in August, naturally). Less than an hour from New York City, the bucolic Stone Barns Center for Food and Agriculture is a wonderful introduction to eating local products. (You can get started immediately at the center's terrific restaurant, Blue Hill.) And a summer afternoon at Iowa's Seed Savers Exchange farm, preserving biodiversity through countless heirloom varieties, might change how you think about fruits and vegetables forever.

321 WATCH A GREEN MOVIE

Lights, camera, (green) action! Invite friends over tonight and check out one of the many films that may educate, inspire, and entertain. Some of the thought-provoking DVDs include *An Inconvenient Truth*, Al Gore's Oscar-winning documentary about global warming; *Syriana*, a political thriller about corruption in the oil industry; and *Erin Brockovich*, which has Julia Roberts taking on a California company polluting a city's water supply. Other possibilities are the fictionalized expose *Fast Food Nation*, the 1979 nuclear power-plant thriller *The China Syndrome*, and the vinyl-siding documentary *Blue Vinyl*. To lighten the mood, try *The Day After Tomorrow,* an action flick dealing with cataclysmic climate change.

322 GO TO A ZOO OR AN AQUARIUM

In recent years, zoos and aquariums have become hip. It's hard not to be dazzled by, say, Baltimore's National Aquarium and its 10,000-plus specimens from all over the world. But even if your local aquarium or zoo isn't that elaborate, remember that taking children to see colorful coral reef fish or a lumbering giant turtle is just about the best way to get them interested in the natural world. Ask about special children's areas, where kids often can touch or feed animals.

The Association of Zoos and Aquariums accredits organizations that meet strict criteria for animal care, conservation, education, and science. For listings, go to aza.org.

323 CAST A GREEN BALLOT

As an educated member of the electorate, you do your research. You find out where the political candidates stand on environmental issues. You may even check voting records to see which ones understand how important a healthy ecosystem is to our future. But you can do more than stepping into a voting booth. Get involved, whether it's at the local level or in a presidential primary. Show campaign support for a party or politician who champions green causes you believe in. By attending rallies, writing letters to your local newspaper, or going door to door to talk with voters, you help raise awareness about issues that affect our well-being. If you're not sure how to get involved, check out the Web site for the League of Conservation Voters (lcv.org). The LCV's mission is "to advocate for sound environmental policies and to elect pro-environmental candidates who will adopt and implement such policies." The site allows you to examine voting records of your representatives in Congress. The LCV helped defeat 9 of 13 "dirty dozen" legislators in the 2006 Congressional elections.

CHAPTER 12

Doing More

Some ways to help the planet don't directly relate to conservation, sustainability, recycling, or any of the other topics discussed so far. Nevertheless, they can make a difference in a world that's sometimes indifferent to global warming, waste, and pollution.

CONTENTS

ECO-FRIENDLY COSMETICS

Many people do not realize the dangers posed, both to themselves and the environment, by the chemicals in cosmetics and personal-care products. Several organizations, including the FDA Cosmetics Information Page (cfsan.fda.gov) and The Campaign for Safe Cosmetics (safecosmetics.org), offer lists of ingredients and products to avoid, along with safe, effective alternatives. Check them out. You will be surprised to find out how many major cosmetic companies have thus far refused to sign the Compact for Safe Cosmetics, which is an agreement not to use chemicals that are known or strongly suspected of causing cancer, mutation, or birth defects in their products.

Be conscious about excessive packaging, too. Among the newest trends are single-dose lip stains and perfumes. Luckily, easy options exist to decrease your impact (and the clutter in your makeup bag). Look for products in recycled packaging. Also take a cue from professional makeup artists: instead of buying individual compacts, choose a refillable palette for your favorite eye shadows, blushes, and bronzers.

One approach to buying green jewelry is to shop for vintage pieces at yard sales, estate auctions, antique stores, and consignment shops.

325 BUY GUILT-FREE JEWELRY

Buying jewelry can damage one's bank account. Extracting precious metals and gems to create jewelry can damage the earth. For example, mining gold to create one 1/3-ounce, 18-karat ring produces about 20 tons of waste. Consider jewelry made from more earth-friendly materials, such as sea glass, shells, stones, and wood. Local artisans can create some incredibly beautiful pieces. Think outside the jewelry box and you can find one-of-a-kind earrings, rings, bracelets, and necklaces made from old coins, keys, and even Scrabble tiles.

If you've got to go for the gold, go easier on the environment by looking for jewelry made from recycled gold. Make sure metals and gems used in any new jewelry come from a sustainable source and are fair-trade certified. To ensure that your money isn't being used to fund wars, avoid blood diamonds. A reputable jeweler should be able to tell you the jewelry's origin.

326 GIVE GREEN GIFTS

Bing Crosby dreamed of a "White Christmas," but we're guessing he'd be OK with a green one, too. To make Christmas (or any gift-giving celebration) greener, try giving eco-friendly gifts. Consider gifts that don't cost a cent. Giving the gift of time (offering a winter's worth of snow shoveling, for example) will keep material goods from ending up in a landfill. Making your own gifts (a birdhouse or cookies, perhaps) or shopping at secondhand stores will cut back on resources, too. Other earth-friendly ideas include canvas grocery bags, organic personal-care products, and jewelry made from recycled materials. Donating to a charity is another possibility, but be aware that some people think giving to a charity should be their choice—and that some teens want iPods in their hands, not donations in their name!

327 BE A GREEN VALENTINE

Have a heart this Valentine's Day and purchase eco-friendly gifts for your loved one. You'll be showing you love the earth, too. Send your sweetheart an e-card or select a card printed on recycled paper. Going with traditional gifts? Make sure those dozen roses come from a local source. (More than 180 million are sold for Valentine's Day each year, and most of them are imported.) Make sure the roses and that box of chocolates are organic, which greatly minimizes the use of pesticides. (Search for organic products by zip code at localharvest.org.)

Do you want to give that special someone something a bit less conventional? Try a heart-shaped beeswax candle, all-natural bath gels, antique jewelry, or a gift certificate for a massage. Use your imagination. Prepare a home-cooked meal with locally grown produce. For more green Valentine's Day gift ideas, check out the Pinks & Blues Green Heart Valentine's gift guide at greenvalentinesguide.com.

Conventional hair dyes pose a possible health risk, are nonrenewable, and flush toxins down the drain each time you dye your hair.

328 GENTLER HAIR COLORING

Perhaps the best approach to eco-friendly hair color is to go natural. The majority of hair dyes, especially those used in salons, are made from petroleum-based ingredients. Meanwhile, natural options, such as vegetable-based dyes and homemade recipes, fade quickly and yield inconsistent results. However, there is a viable option. Aveda Salons (aveda.com) offer dyes that are 99-percent plant derived and permanent dyes that are 97-percent plant based. The results are natural looking and consistent. Aveda also offers cost-friendly options for customers at their institutes around the country.

329 WEAR NATURAL CLOTHES

According to the Sustainable Cotton Project, one-third of a pound of synthetic fertilizers and chemicals is required to manufacture a single cotton T-shirt.

Manufacturing clothes, especially those made from petroleum-based synthetics such as nylon and polyester, takes its toll on the environment. Show style while practicing consciousness by purchasing clothes made from natural fibers such as organic cotton, hemp, bamboo, soy, and wool. Processing natural fibers into organic clothing is done using little or no chemicals, minimizing the damage to our natural resources. According to the Sustainable Cotton Project, cotton crops account for 25 percent of all pesticides used in the United States. Organic cotton is grown without the chemical fertilizers and pesticides.

330 VOLUNTEER VACATIONS

It's vacation time! Europe is nice. So are tropical beaches. But how about visiting an exotic locale and doing more than sightseeing and sunbathing? Work on an organic farm in Hawaii. Help with a sea turtle conservation project in Costa Rica. Assist an archaeological dig in Egypt. Create habitat for native plants and animals in Australia. Rebuild homes along the Gulf Coast. Numerous options are available online. Try sierraclub.org to get started. Enjoy yourself while helping the planet.

331 SUPPORT GREEN COMPANIES

Although many corporations now support green initiatives for marketing reasons, it's no reason not to reward their good behavior. The question is, which ones are making a real difference and which only pay lip service. One way to find out is to check out the Ceres-ACCA award winners at ceres.org. Ceres-ACCA recognizes companies and organizations that are making sustainable manufacturing a priority. Some recent winners include Bristol-Myers Squibb, Nike, and Hewlett-Packard.

332 GREEN INVESTING

So you are making every effort to maintain a healthy personal relationship with nature. However, there is one thing you may be missing. If you are investing in companies that are responsible for pollution or other practices destructive to the environment, your money could be working against you. Make it work for you by investing in green companies, such as those that focus on organic foods and renewable energy.

Well-run, socially responsible funds exist but are difficult to find. Therefore, experts suggest a three-pronged strategy when choosing to invest green. First, search out green companies. Next, look at "clean" companies—those that do not have a detrimental effect on the environment. Stocks in healthcare, software, and the service sector are often good options. Finally, if you own stock in a polluting corporation, let them know that you would like to see them develop a better environmental policy.

333 STAY ON TRAILS

When you go hiking, you're a guest in the home of plants and animals, so be respectful. Stay on trails. If you go off a trail, you can cause erosion. You could also step on—and kill—insects, small animals, and plants. Trampling plants takes away food for deer and other creatures. Don't take a shortcut, cut a switchback, or blaze a new trail, even if the one you're on is a bit muddy—your shoes will dry in a day, but stepped-on plants will take years to recover. Staying on trails keeps human impact to a minimum. It's safer, too, because you're less likely to get bitten by a snake, get poison ivy, or get lost.

If you're on a trail that allows dogs, keep your canine on a leash.

334 BE A LIGHT TRAVELER

Our efforts to live responsibly shouldn't take a vacation, even when we do. To minimize the impact of travel, consider staying close to home for your next vacation. The less pollution-causing travel involved, the better. If you must travel by plane, fly with an airline that does its part to protect the environment. The same goes for lodging; check greenhotels.com to see if a hotel is a member of the Green Hotels Association. Let the hotel know it's unnecessary to clean the towels and linens every day, and turn off the lights, TV, and air conditioning/heat when you leave your room. Walk and use public transportation as often as possible.

Get a true flavor for the place you're visiting by eating local foods. Do lots of low-impact activities, such as hiking, biking, and kayaking. Finally, try to resist the kitschy souvenirs. Bring home artwork or jewelry from a local artisan, a postcard or two, museum ticket stubs, a matchbook from a great restaurant, digital photos, and wonderful memories.

335 ENVIRONMENTAL GRILLING

Eight out of every 10 households in the United States own a grill. When these folks are lighting up the grill at the same time, that's quite an environmental impact. To lessen the harmful effects associated with grilling, start by buying a durable grill instead of a cheap model that must be replaced every few years. This will leave a smaller ecological footprint. The most popular fuel options are gas or charcoal. Gas grills, despite using nonrenewable petroleum, are a friendlier environmental choice. They burn cleaner and don't contribute to deforestation. If you grill with charcoal, avoid conventional briquettes, which contain hazardous ingredients (including coal dust) and give off carbon dioxide. Look for lump charcoal from a sustainable source instead. Pellet grills (small wood pellets provide the fuel source) are increasing in popularity thanks to their energy efficiency and their clean-burning properties, though grills are not widely available yet. Electric grills have the least environmental impact, but they can be difficult to find, and many argue that the flavor an electric grill imparts doesn't come close to what a charcoal or gas model produces.

336 UNMASK HALLOWEEN

Halloween is a fun time for the kids, but it's not so fun for the earth—the billions spent each year on costumes, candy, and decorations create scary amounts of waste. Do your part to make each October 31 a bit more eco-friendly. Don't buy a costume that will be used for only one night; instead, make your own using what you've got in the house or what you can find at a thrift store. (A number of Web sites have terrific ideas for homemade costumes.) Accessorize with a reusable goody-gathering bag. Nothing beats a pillowcase. And don't drive your child door to door— walk the neighborhood.

It's tough to come up with healthy alternatives for young trick-or-treaters who want candy and will be angry or upset if they don't get it, but it can be done. Give out fair-trade chocolates. Consider nonedible options, as well, such as comics, bubbles, and stickers.

Skip the store-bought decorations and get creative with what you've got. For example, empty boxes can easily become tombstones. And don't forget the locally grown pumpkins, of course. They will add a nice finishing touch, and come November you can make pumpkin pies, roast the seeds, and compost the rest.

337 GIVE TO A GREEN CHARITY

We share our hard-earned money with those that are important to us. We tithe at church. We support cancer research. We give money to our alma mater. We should earmark a portion of our annual charity budget for environmental causes, too. Our donations don't have to be monetary; they can come in the form of time, food, or goods (computers, clothes, cell phones, and so forth). But money helps to plant trees, clean air, conserve wetlands, protect wildlife, and support other worthy causes. A great way to support a favorite cause *and* stay in shape is to participate in a fundraising walk, run, or ride.

Environmental organizations large and small are always in need of charity. Some of the bigger groups include The Nature Conservancy, Heifer International, and the World Wildlife Fund. Do your research: you want to make sure the organization is legit and that most of your money is going directly toward the cause.

Oh, one more thing: did you know you could give to charity by simply searching the Internet? Check out search engines such as GoodSearch and Searchgive, which donate a portion of their advertising revenues to charity.

338 SPAY OR NEUTER YOUR PET

According to The Humane Society of the United States, 70,000 puppies and kittens are born every day—much greater than the human birth rate. Millions of them end up in already overburdened shelters, and most of them are killed. By having your pet spayed or neutered, you'll control the population, which means fewer unwanted animals and fewer resources (food, water, vaccinations, and so forth) devoted to their care.

You'll help Fluffy and Rocky, too, because spaying and neutering eliminates or reduces the risk of developing health problems, including testicular, ovarian, prostate, and breast cancer.

339 KEEP HONEYBEES

Keeping honeybees is a rewarding hobby that will help increase your local bee population and provide all the honey you can use. A wooden beehive can be purchased in kit form. A honeybee colony, consisting of workers, drones, and one queen bee, can be ordered by mail or purchased from a local beekeeper in early spring. Put the hive in a sunny spot. Put the bees in the hive on a warm sunny day and they'll instinctively begin their foraging activities while the queen begins to lay eggs. For routine hive inspections, you'll need a protective veil, gloves, a hive tool, and a smoker to calm the bees.

Honey harvest begins late in the summer and is the sweetest part of the job.

340 SUSTAINABLE WEDDINGS

You're engaged. Congratulations! Begin your new life together by planning environmentally friendly nuptials. There are plenty of ways to do it. Here are 10.

• **Have the wedding outdoors,** perhaps at a botanical garden, nature preserve, or beach. If possible, have the ceremony and reception at the same spot.

• **Use 100-percent recycled stationery** when creating your invitations.

• **Set up a Web site** to have people RSVP online. It can also include directions, nearby hotels, and local events.

• **Select a vintage dress**—or one you'll wear more than once.

• **Encourage guests to carpool** or use public transportation.

• **Use a local florist,** and donate the flowers to a hospital or nursing home when you're through.

• **Plan a menu of locally grown foods,** and donate leftovers to a food kitchen or homeless shelter.

• **Use real plates,** glasses, silverware, and linens instead of disposables.

• **Choose digital photography.**

• **Give eco-friendly favors,** such as organic chocolates or natural soaps.

Sailboats are far more environmentally friendly than motor boats, for obvious reasons, but regardless of your choice of boat, practice kind stewardship of the sea.

341 CLEANER BOATING

Show some nautical know-how by following environmentally friendly boating practices. Increase your boat's fuel efficiency by keeping the engine tuned, the bottom free of debris, and the load light—keep bilges dry and bring only what's necessary. To keep fuel in the tank and not in the water, refuel slowly and use absorbent pads or rags to catch drips and spills. Use nontoxic paints and coatings on the hull to control biofouling. (See epaint.com.) Look for nontoxic cleaning products that are free of phosphates, and handle the majority of cleaning jobs—especially the big ones—when the boat is on land. Never throw anything overboard. Wait until you're onshore to get rid of garbage, recyclables, and hazardous waste. One such waste is sewage. Manage yours responsibly. Use marine pump-out stations, where possible, and do not dump untreated sewage in coastal and inland waters. To avoid the pump-out system, consider the Air Head Dry Toilet. (See airheadtoilet.com.) Do your part the next time you set sail because we're all in the same boat.

342 FRIENDLIER FISHING

It's not too difficult to be a responsible, ethical fisherman. You can start by not fishing for species that are threatened or endangered. And get the lead out— use sinkers and jigs, which are often lost at the bottom of your favorite fishing hole, that are lead free. Try a lure made from recycled bottle caps. (See bottle-caplure.com.) Consider stopping catch-and-release fishing, which is cruel. (How'd you like to be hooked and then let go?) If you won't fish only for what you'll eat, at least practice CPR (Catch, Photograph, Release) as quickly and gently as possible. Obey all size and bag limits; they ensure a better opportunity for fish to reproduce and maintain stable populations.

343 BE A GREENER CAMPER

Are we ever more aware—and more appreciative—of our surroundings than when we're camping under the stars? Show your appreciation by being an eco-friendly camper. Look for camping apparel and equipment made from recycled materials or earth-friendly materials, such as hemp. Be mindful of where you walk so you don't step on small creatures or trample plants. Avoid dishes and cutlery that are disposable. Cook your food on a small stove—using some fuel is better than burning deadwood that insects and small animals call home. If you must build a campfire, keep it under control and make sure you put it out completely. Don't light a fire when it's windy, and never leave a fire unattended. Don't wash things (including yourself) or go to the bathroom anywhere near a water source. Leave no trace that you were ever there—pick up your trash and recyclables, and take out what you bring in, including toilet paper.

You won't have to leave all comforts behind. Biome Lifestyle (biomelifestyle.com) offers an "Eco-Camp Kit" that includes a water-powered alarm clock, solar-powered iPod charger, organic cotton roll-up bed, self-powered LED lantern, and organic soap.

344 HOST A GREENER BIRTHDAY PARTY

Get creative and find ways to lighten your impact when it's time for your child to blow out the birthday candles. Invite people by phone, e-mail, or the Internet. Serve fresh, locally produced foods. Avoid disposable tablecloths, napkins, plates, cups, and utensils.

Your child probably has enough toys already, so request movie tickets, museum passes, and other items that won't take up space. In lieu of gifts, have guests bring gently used toys and books to donate to less fortunate children. Don't send guests on their way

with a goody-bag filled with candy and plastic trinkets. Provide more thoughtful favors, such as tree seed kits. (See treeinabox.com.).

345 CHOOSE AN ECO LODGE

Going skiing? Reduce carbon emissions by choosing a nearby resort and traveling by train instead of jetting off to the Swiss Alps. Look for a ski area that follows green practices, such as providing public transportation, encouraging recycling, avoiding artificial snowmaking, and using renewable energy. Many ski resorts do their part to fight global warming. They understand it can lead to shorter seasons and less snow. The Canyons Resort in Park City, Utah, uses solar-powered lighting. In Wyoming, the Jackson Hole Mountain Resort powers two of its lifts with wind power. Use the scorecard created by the advocacy group Ski Area Citizens' Coalition (skiareacitizens.com), which grades Western U.S. resorts on environmental policies and practices, including energy efficiency, water conservation, and wildlife protection. You could always try cross-country skiing, which is environmentally friendlier than the downhill variety because there are no graded slopes, cleared trees, or ski lifts.

346 HAVE A GREEN FOURTH

Celebrate Independence Day by taking small steps to reduce our nation's dependence on energy. Hosting a cookout? Buy local foods, and follow the grilling tips found on page 230. Use reusable plates, cups, and utensils. Going to the beach? Walk or bike there, if possible. Use an organic sunscreen with few, if any, chemicals, and be sure to pick up any litter you generate. Watching a fireworks display? It may be beautiful, but it's a big-time enemy of the environment. The smoke and dust that are produced during one of these pyrotechnic shows pollute the air, the water, and the ground. The holiday isn't going to go sans fireworks anytime soon, but perhaps there's a concert or block party you can attend instead.

347 HAVE A GREEN THANKSGIVING

Your aunt's delicious green-bean casserole doesn't have to be the only way you "green up" your Thanksgiving. If you'll be spending the holiday away from home, consider mass transit. Fewer greenhouse gases equal cleaner air.

Eating a soy or tofu turkey may be too drastic a change for the traditionalists in the family, but you can go with an organic, farm-raised turkey that isn't full of pesticides. Use locally grown veggies, which save the gas burned when items are shipped to market, and serve some organic wine or beer.

Skip plastic and paper. Use nondisposable or biodegradable plates and utensils, along with cloth napkins. And don't let leftovers go to waste. Send them home with guests or donate them to a shelter or food pantry. Finally, decorate with gourds, dried flowers, pinecones, and other natural items.

348 MAKE A RESOLUTION

After counting down from 10, sipping some champagne, and belting out a chorus or two of "Auld Lang Syne," it's time to make a New Year's resolution. This time, don't just make—and probably break before the year has hardly begun—the ones made over and over again. In addition to the usual assortment (eat healthier, exercise more, spend more time with friends), make a resolution to live a greener life. Start small, so you don't drop the ball before the next ball drops in Times Square.

349 PROTECT YOUR SCALP

Having a bad hair day? It may be because of your shampoo. Have you ever taken a look at the labels on the most popular shampoo brands? Many of them contain some scary ingredients that may be stripping your hair of its natural oils. To keep sodium lauryl sulfate and other chemicals off your scalp, try a less toxic alternative. More and more companies have come out with natural hair products that are derived from plants and organic ingredients. A quick Internet search will come up with many natural products that are free of synthetic fragrances. (Try burtsbees.com and lush.com.) If you

LUSH (lush.com) sells natural shampoos with essential oils and eco-friendly shampoo bars that require no packaging.

are game enough to try a scalp "mud bath," so to speak, there are all-natural, clay-based hair products that don't contain any soap or foaming agents. (See terresentials.com.) Some folks shun commercial shampoos and instead use apple cider vinegar or baking soda.

350 GET A GREEN CREDIT CARD

Reducing consumption is a great way to go green. When you must buy something, use a credit card that allows you to donate a percentage of your purchases to an environmental cause or group, or earn points toward green products and services. The Brighter Planet Visa (issued by Bank of America) and the Earth Rewards MasterCard

(General Electric) are two examples of credit cards that offer carbon offsets. Users donate a percentage of their purchases to fight global warming. Affinity cards, such as the Working Assets Visa (MBNA), provide donations to the charity or nonprofit whose logo appears on the card. Find a credit card with a green angle that suits you, and make sure it isn't backed by a company whose practices you deem eco-unfriendly.

351 RENT OUT A ROOM

Sharing is caring, right? Well, you can show you care about the planet by sharing your home with a roomer. Renting out a spare room to, say, a graduate student or a businessman looking to live close to work on weekdays is a terrific way to maximize resources and live lighter. The roomer will use less energy and will generate less waste than he or she would if he or she were living alone. You'll earn some extra money. Just be careful and take any necessary precautions before opening your home to a stranger.

352 KEEP CHRISTMAS GREEN

It's not easy being green at Christmas, a time when consumerism runs amok. Fortunately, there are a number of things—many of them discussed throughout this book—you can do.

• **Decorate with energy-efficient** Christmas lights.

• **Choose a real tree** over an artificial one. Real trees are recyclable and not made with petroleum. If possible, purchase a living tree instead of one that's been cut.

• **Send e-cards.**

• **Bring your own bag** to the store when shopping for gifts.

• **Give eco-friendly gifts.**

• **Get creative** when it comes to wrapping those gifts.

• **Buy locally** produced food for Christmas dinner and locally produced craft items as gifts.

• **Donate any extra food** to a soup kitchen or shelter.

• **Burn beeswax** or soy candles.

• **Avoid disposable items** (plastic flatware, foam cups, paper napkins, and so forth) when hosting a meal.

• **Recycle your Christmas cards.**

• **Plant your tree.** According to liveearth.org, a single tree can absorb more than one ton of CO_2 over its lifetime.

353 PLAY CARD OR BOARD GAMES

There's no law that states the TV or computer must get turned on each evening. So, every so often, try something that requires not a single kilowatt of electricity: play a card game or board game. You'll have fun and build bonds, and—depending on which game you choose—you may even keep your mind sharp! Popular card games include poker, rummy, and bridge. Monopoly, Life, Risk, Clue, and Trivial Pursuit are some of the top board games. Don't forget about chess, dominoes, and Scrabble, too. There's even an environmental board game called Save the Whales in which players try to save whales from oil spills, hunters, and other dangers. (You can order a copy at childandnature.com.) Consider instituting a weekly "Game Night," and have a different family member choose the game each week. Battling family and friends at cards or a board game is a small step in the battle against global warming.

Play games that demand brain power, not silicone chips and electricity.

354 PLAN A GREEN FAREWELL

A funeral is hardly green. You can't avoid damaging the environment when you embalm bodies, bury those bodies in laminated caskets, and chemically treat the cemetery lawns. Cremation is better for the earth, even though it requires the use of fossil fuels and releases CO_2, because it saves resources and land. An even more eco-friendly option is a natural, or green, burial. A person is buried in a biodegradable coffin and decomposes naturally, returning to the earth in "dust to dust" fashion. No chemicals are used. No waste is created.

355 VOLUNTEER FOR A GREEN CAUSE

Make a difference. Assist in a beach cleanup. Spend a few afternoons each week at an animal shelter. Help staff an information table at an Earth Day event. Serve as a guide at a state park. Teach kids at a local school about the environment. Plant flowers at a project site. Educate shoppers at a farmers' market about recycling and composting. All you need is interest, enthusiasm, and time. Volunteering is a great way to show a commitment to a cause or belief, explore personal interests, share a skill, and make new friends

Become part of a Green Team today. Check idealist.org, greenvolunteers.com, and other Web sites for volunteer opportunities.

356 PAINT A PRETTY PICTURE

Exposure to the chemicals found in some art supplies can lead to an assortment of acute or chronic health problems, with children being particularly vulnerable. Look for safer alternatives prior to starting your next masterpiece. Many artists use acrylic paints because they dry faster than oil paints and do not require toxic solvents, such as turpentine, to thin the paints or for cleanup. Water-soluble oil paints do exist, though what may be most important from an environmental standpoint is the pigment. Pigments in art paints often contain cadmium, lead, and other toxic metals. Nontoxic pigment options are available. (Check out earthpigments.com.) Whenever you purchase art paint, look for the Art & Creative Materials Institute's AP (Approved Product) label, which certifies that it contains no materials in sufficient quantities to be toxic to humans.

To find out what chemicals are in a given art-supply product, check its Materials Safety Data Sheet, which can be obtained from the manufacturer.

357 HAVE A GREEN WORKOUT

Working out makes you feel better, but it may be hurting the environment. Try staying fit and treating the earth well at the same time. You can have a great workout sans machines, so don't hop in the carbon-spewing car and drive to an air-conditioned gym filled with electricity-consuming treadmills. Stay home with a workout DVD or, better still, head outside—after changing into eco-friendly workout gear made from recycled material or eco-friendly material, such as organic cotton. Perform push-ups on a bench. Try standing calf raises on a curb. Do hanging crunches on the monkey bars. Chase a Frisbee on the beach. Join a local sports league. Go hiking. None of these activities require a gym membership.

If you are heading to the gym, jog or bike there, weather permitting. Instead of buying bottled water, bring a reusable water bottle or drink from the gym's fountain. When your sneakers get old, recycle them. Programs such as Nike's Reuse-A-Shoe (letmeplay.com/reuseashoe) will process the materials and use them for various sports surfaces.

358 READ AN E-BOOK

Some bibliophiles will never be able to get rid of printed books. Fair enough. But if you believe the words are more important than the medium, consider an electronic book (e-book), which is read on a computer or an e-book reader. No trees are killed to make an e-book, and pollution-causing paper and inks are avoided. E-books also require much less physical space; hundreds of books can be stored on a reader, such as the Amazon Kindle or Sony Reader.

E-books are cheaper than traditional books, and the text size can be adjusted, making every book a large-type edition. Built-in search functions and dictionaries and improved outdoor readability are other pluses. The minuses? The reading devices are made with plastics and metals, require power to read, and cost a few hundred dollars (so don't drop them!). And many books are not available in digital format. Not ready for e-reading? Buy books printed on recycled paper or paper that has Forest Stewardship Council (FSC) certification.

359 HUNT RESPONSIBLY

Hunting may not seem like a topic for this book, but it can be beneficial, and it should be done in an environmentally friendly manner. Hunting for food means you don't have to buy packaged meat that comes from force-fed animals and has been processed and shipped. Hunting overpopulated animals is a form of wildlife management and can have health factors. (In Connecticut, hunting deer helps reduce the spread of Lyme disease.) Hunt in season only where permissible, and don't hunt protected, threatened, or endangered species. Consider hunting with a bow instead of a shotgun or rifle.

Avoid the abhorrent practice of trophy hunting. Think about getting the thrill without the kill by trying "green hunting," or "eco-hunting," in which lions, elephants, and other big game are shot with tranquilizer darts. Researchers take blood and examine the animal while it's unconscious. We don't recommend traumatizing an animal via immobilization, but it is better than killing for sport. If you must have a trophy head mounted on your wall, we suggest one made from 100 percent recyclable cardboard. (See cardboardsafari.com.)

360 BELL YOUR CAT

There are more than 66 million pet cats in the United States. And cats, by nature, are predators. They stalk. They pounce. They kill. The best way to protect birds and small animals is to keep your beloved feline indoors or build an outdoor enclosure. If these are not options for you, put a bell on your cat's collar. A belled collar isn't foolproof, but it will help warn animals of a cat's approach and save the lives of millions of birds.

361 GIVE ME A "G"

There are many factors in deciding what university to attend. Add one more to the list: green practices. When investing in your future, invest in a college that is committed to helping the environment. Find out what prospective schools do when it comes to organic food, energy use and renewable energy, recycling, waste reduction, cleaner transportation, green building, and other environmental issues that are important to you.

Here's a view of what's happening on eco-friendly campuses across the country: the University of Pennsylvania purchases food from local producers, offers fair-trade and organic products, and uses biodegradable to-go containers in the dining halls. St. Olaf College in Minnesota produces much of its own electricity with a wind turbine. The University of Virginia uses 30 biodiesel buses. The University of Florida has five LEED-certified buildings and requires that all new buildings be LEED-certified.

362 MAKE A CAREER OF IT

So you thought you already were "getting in the green." Well, maybe not yet. The phrase refers specifically to taking a green career path. A green job refers to any position within a company that's actively trying to reduce human impact on the environment or helping to restore it. These include industries such as organic foods and consumer products, energy conservation, renewable energy, green building, environmental cleanup, socially-responsible investing, sustainable tourism, and nonprofit environmental advocacy. In fact, a quick online search for "green careers" yields opportunities in almost any field, along with organizations willing to aid with the transition from your current job.

If you are still a student, begin preparing for a green career, regardless of your major. Look into an independent study with a professor doing environmental research in a discipline of your choice. Explore internships with green companies. And get active in your community.

363 PRACTICE GREEN SEX

Yep, we can be passionate about the planet while being passionate in the bedroom. Get in the mood by lighting some beeswax or soy wax candles, giving a massage (use organic oils, of course), or uncorking a bottle of organic wine. Turn on your significant other by donning some sexy, sustainable underwear or lingerie made from organic cotton or hemp silk. Make love on a bed with bamboo sheets. (See page 82.) If you're using a lubricant, avoid petroleum-based products—all-natural and organic lubes are available. Men, use latex condoms and dispose of them in the trash, not the toilet.

If you still haven't found your green lover, you can look for one at an eco-related matchmaking Web site, such as greensingles.com or green-passions.com.

364 DON'T BE A LITTERBUG

Litter is everywhere. Syringes and broken glass at the beach are dangerous to people. Cigarette butts on the side of the road release toxic chemicals when they break down. Plastic bags in parking lots endanger birds that mistake them for food, choke, and die. The next time you're in possession of a candy wrapper, empty soda can, or advertising flyer, find a trash can—it's not that difficult to do. Being sanitary shows sanity.

365 SHARE THIS BOOK

Well, 364 entries down, one to go. At this point, you're well aware of the "reduce, reuse, recycle" mantra, and you're gung-ho about helping the planet. You can make a difference, and it begins now. Share this book. For sales reasons, we'd love it if you purchased copies of this book for all your friends, but it's even greener to put what you've learned into action and pass along this now gently used copy to a friend.

The following list of manufacturers and associations is meant to be a general guide to additional industry and product-related sources. It is not intended as a listing of products and manufacturers represented by the text or photographs in this book.

American Community Gardening Association

1777 E. Broad St.
Columbus, OH 43203
877-275-2242
www.communitygarden.org
A nonprofit membership organization whose mission is to build community by increasing and enhancing community gardening and greening across the United States and Canada.

American Council for an Energy-Efficient Economy

1001 Connecticut Ave. NW, Ste. 801
Washington, DC 20036
202-429°8873
www.aceee.org
A nonprofit organization dedicated to advancing energy efficiency as a means of promoting both economic prosperity and environmental protection.

The Arbor Day Foundation

100 Arbor Ave.
Nebraska City, NE 68410
888-448-7337
www.arborday.org
An organization that helps people plant and care for trees in an effort to advance rural land conservation and forest stewardship. The Arbor Day Foundation promotes rain forest preservation and tree planting.

Blue Ocean Institute

Muttontown Park and Preserve
Chelsea Mansion
34 Muttontown Ln.
East Norwich, NY 11732
516-922-9500
www.blueocean.org
A nonprofit conservation organization that uses science, art, and literature to inspire a closer relationship with the sea and devise practical solutions to conservation problems.

Consumer Product Safety Commission

4330 East West Hwy.
Bethesda, MD 20814
800-638-2772
www.cpsc.gov
An organization charged with protecting the public from unreasonable risks of serious injury or death from more than 15,000 types of consumer products.

Department of Agriculture

1400 Independence Ave. SW
Washington, DC 20250
202-720-9305
www.usda.gov
A federal organization that develops and executes policy on farming, agriculture, and food. The USDA's National Organic Program governs organic certification and assures consumers that the foods they purchase are produced, processed, and certified to be consistent with national organic standards.

Department of Energy

1000 Independence Ave. SW
Washington, DC 20585
800-342-5363
www.doe.gov
A federal organization that promotes America's energy security through reliable, clean, and affordable energy. The DOE Web site has free material focused on energy consumption and energy efficiency.

Direct Marketing Association

1120 Avenue of the Americas
New York, NY 10036-6700
212-768-7277

www.dmachoice.org

A trade association of businesses and non-profit organizations that advocates industry standards for responsible marketing. The DMA's Mail Preference Service helps consumers reduce the amount of commercial or nonprofit mail they receive at home.

Earth 911

14646 N. Kierland Blvd., Ste. 100
Scottsdale, AZ 85254
480-889-2650
http://earth911.org

A Web-based environmental company that provides information on recycling and responsible, sustainable consumption. The site allows you to find a local recycling or reuse location for batteries, paint, electronics, and more by inputting your zip code.

Energy Star

1200 Pennsylvania Ave. NW
Washington, DC 20460
888-782-7937
www.energystar.gov

A joint program of the Environmental Protection Agency and Department of Energy that offers energy-efficient solutions. Appliances that have earned the Energy Star label use less energy, save money, and help protect the environment.

Environmental Protection Agency

Ariel Rios Building
1200 Pennsylvania Ave. NW
Washington, DC 20460
202-272-0167
www.epa.gov

A federal agency committed to protecting human health and the environment. The EPA's Web site includes a wealth of information on environmental toxins, indoor air quality, and household hazardous waste.

Environmental Working Group

1436 U St. NW, Ste. 100

Washington, DC 20009
202-667-6982
www.ewg.org

A nonprofit organization with a mission to use the power of public information to protect public health and the environment. The EWG is an excellent resource for information on toxins in household and beauty products.

The Food and Drug Administration

5600 Fishers Ln.
Rockville, MD 20857
888-463-6332
www.fda.gov

A federal agency that protects and promotes public health by assuring the safety, efficacy, and security of various products, including drugs, foods, and cosmetics.

Forest Stewardship Council – U.S.

1155 30th St. NW, Ste. 300
Washington, DC 20007
202-342-0413
www.fscus.org

The U.S. chapter of an international organization created to promote responsible management of forests worldwide. The Web site includes information on policies, standards, and certification regarding forestry policies.

The Freecycle Network

P.O. Box 294
Tucson, AZ 85702
www.freecycle.org

A private, nonprofit organization with more than 4 million members worldwide that, in an effort to reduce waste, save precious resources, and ease the burden on landfills, give away (and receive) old items instead of discarding them.

Goodwill Industries International

15810 Indianola Dr.
Rockville, MD 20855
800-741-0186
www.goodwill.org

A nonprofit membership organization that provides education, training, and career services for people with disadvantages. The revenues from clothing and household goods donated and sold at Goodwill stores nationwide fund the organization's services.

Green Hotels Association
P.O. Box 420212
Houston, TX 77242-0212
713-789-8889
www.greenhotels.com
An organization that encourages, promotes, and supports environmental practices in the lodging and hospitality industry. The Web site includes tips on how to save water, save energy, and reduce waste while traveling.

Habitat for Humanity International
121 Habitat St.
Americus, GA 31709-3498
800-422-4828
www.habitat.org
A nonprofit, ecumenical Christian housing ministry that seeks to eliminate poverty housing and homelessness. Volunteers have helped to build more than 250,000 houses around the world for families in need.

Healthy Building Network
Institute for Local Self-Reliance
927 15th St. NW, 4th Floor
Washington, DC 20005
202-898-1610
www.healthybuilding.net
A network of green building professionals, health activists, and others who are interested in promoting healthier building materials as a means of improving public health and preserving the global environment.

League of Conservation Voters
1920 L St. NW, Ste. 800
Washington, DC 20036
202-785-8683
www.lcv.org

An independent political voice for the environment. The LCV elevates the profile of environmental politics and holds elected officials accountable on conservation issues. You can check candidates' positions on environmental issues through the LCV's National Environmental Scorecard.

LocalHarvest
220 21st Ave.
Santa Cruz, CA 95062
831-475-8150
www.localharvest.org
A Web site that provides a nationwide directory of locally grown food. A search engine helps you find small farms, farmers' markets, co-ops, restaurants, and other sources of sustainably grown food in your area.

Marine Stewardship Council
2110 N. Pacific St., Ste. 102
Seattle, WA 98103
206-691-0188
www.msc.org
An independent, nonprofit organization that promotes sustainable fisheries and responsible fishing practices. The MSC rewards fisheries that meet its environmental standard with a distinctive blue product label.

National Lead Information Center
422 S. Clinton Ave.
Rochester, NY 14620
800-424-5323
www.epa.gov/lead/pubs/nlic.htm
A resource that provides information about lead hazards and their prevention. The NLIC operates under a contract with the Environmental Protection Agency.

National Resources Defense Council
40 W. 20th St.
New York, NY 10011
212-727-2700
www.nrdc.org
An environmental action organization

whose mission is to protect wildlife and to ensure a safe and healthy environment for all living things. The Web site's "Green Living" section offers guides to saving energy, conserving resources, and more.

National Turfgrass Evaluation Program
Beltsville Agricultural Research Center West
10300 Baltimore Ave.
Bldg. 003, Rm. 218
Beltsville, MD 20705
301-504-5125
www.ntep.org
A research program that tests, evaluates, and identifies turfgrass species in the United States and Canada. NTEP data is used to find environmentally sound turfgrasses.

The Nature Conservancy
4245 N. Fairfax Dr., Ste. 100
Arlington, VA 22203-1606
800-628-6860
www.nature.org
A conservation organization that works to protect ecologically important lands and waters for nature and people. It has protected more than 117 million acres of land.

Ocean Conservancy
1300 19th St. NW, 8th Floor
Washington, DC 20036
800-519-1541
www.oceanconservancy.org
A conservation organization that promotes healthy and diverse ocean ecosystems and opposes practices that threaten ocean life.

The Salvation Army
615 Slaters Ln.
P.O. Box 269
Alexandria, VA 22313
www.salvationarmyusa.org
A nonprofit Christian organization well known for its charitable efforts and social services, including disaster relief. The sale of donated items at Salvation Army thrift stores

goes to support the organization's addiction recovery programs.

Sustainable Cotton Project
P.O. Box 363
Davis, CA 95617
530-756-8518 ext. 34
www.sustainablecotton.org
An organization focused on the production and use of cotton. The SCP is committed to creating a cleaner cotton industry and to promoting fair-trade organic and sustainable cotton clothes.

Sustainable Forestry Initiative
1600 Wilson Blvd., Ste. 810
Arlington, VA 22209
703-875-9500
www.aboutsfi.org
An independent forest certification program. SFI conducts site visits and chain-of-custody audits to ensure wood is grown and harvested in an earth-friendly manner.

U.S. Green Building Council
1800 Massachusetts Ave. NW, Ste. 300
Washington, DC 20036
800-795-1747
www.usgbc.org
A nonprofit organization that certifies sustainable homes, businesses, hospitals, and schools. The USGBC created and oversees the LEED (see Glossary) rating system for homes and commercial buildings.

World Wildlife Fund
1250 24th St. NW
P.O. Box 97180
Washington, DC 20090-7180
202-293-4800
www.wwf.org
A multinational conservation organization that works to protect natural areas, save endangered species, and address threats to the health of ecological systems, such as global warming and pollution.

Biodegradable Capable of being broken down by living things and absorbed into the ecosystem.

Biodiesel A clean-burning fuel derived from renewable resources, such as vegetable oils and animal fats.

Biofuel Fuel derived from biodegradable, renewable resources, such as wood, plants, and grains.

Carbon footprint An estimated measure of the amount of carbon dioxide and other greenhouse gases emitted by businesses or organizations as part of their day-to-day operations or by individuals as part of their daily activities.

Daylighting The use of natural light from windows, skylights, and other openings to supplement or replace electric light in a home or building.

Ecosystem A set of living things interacting with one another and their physical environment, functioning as a unit.

Embodied energy The amount of energy required to bring a product, material, or service to the point of use, including the energy used during extraction, manufacturing, packaging, transportation, assembly, and installation.

Essential oils Oils used for their aroma and for medicinal purposes. Natural essential oils (made from lemons, peppermint leaves, lavender, and so forth) are safer than artificial fragrances.

Fair trade A trading partnership that seeks better social and environmental standards for disadvantaged producers and workers and advocates the fair payment for the purchase of their goods, particularly those exported from developing countries.

Fossil fuel Fuel formed in the earth from ancient (fossilized) plant or animal remains. Fossil fuels, such as coal, oil, or natural gas, were created millions of years ago, and more can't be produced when we run out. Burning fossil fuels generates greenhouse gases.

Geothermal Relating to heat from the earth. Geothermal power is clean, safe energy generated by this naturally occurring heat, which is stored beneath the earth's surface.

Global warming An increase in the earth's average atmospheric and oceanic temperatures that is believed to be the result of an increase in the greenhouse effect, resulting especially from pollution.

Gray water Household wastewater (from a sink, for example) that does not contain serious contaminants.

Greenhouse gas Gas caused by the greenhouse effect, which is the warming of the surface and atmosphere of the earth that is caused by conversion of solar radiation into heat.

High-efficiency particulate air (HEPA) filters Filters, typically found in vacuums and air-conditioning units, that are designed to remove more than 99 percent of harmful allergens from the air. They help reduce dust, mold spores, pet dander, and other allergens.

Hybrid A car that is powered by more than one energy source. A hybrid most often refers to a car that combines an internal combustion engine and an electric motor powered by batteries.

Integrated Pest Management (IPM) A method of pest control that keeps insects, diseases, and weeds at tolerable levels using the least-toxic methods available.

LED lighting Long-lasting lighting that conserves electricity. LED stands for light-emitting diode.

LEED Abbreviation for Leadership in Energy and Environmental Design, a U.S. Green Building Council program that evaluates the environmental sustainability of buildings and certifies them based on the number of points earned.

Microfiber A nonabrasive synthetic material (a blend of polyester and polyamide) that removes dust, dirt, and grease from any hard surface, including mirrors and countertops, without streaking, scratching, or leaving lint.

Organic Relating to or derived from living organisms. Organic refers to the way agricultural products are produced and processed. To be labeled organic, an item must meet certain standards set by the USDA. Crops must be produced without the use of pesticides and other synthetic chemicals and processed without food additives. Organic meat, poultry, eggs, and dairy products must come from animals that are reared without antibiotics and growth hormones.

Passive solar Refers to capitalizing on the sun's energy to heat and cool living spaces naturally, without the use of mechanical or electrical devices. Passive solar design takes advantage of the sun through simple things such as strategically placed windows for lighting and cross-ventilation purposes; floors and interior walls made of thermal mass material, such as brick or concrete, that absorb and hold the sun's radiant heat; overhangs, awnings, blinds, and trees to provide shade; and light paint colors to reflect the sun's heat.

Pesticide A poisonous chemical solution used to kill ants, spiders, roaches, and other household pests.

Petrochemical A chemical derived from petroleum or natural gas. Products made from petrochemicals include plastics, detergents, solvents, and flooring and insulation materials.

Petroleum based Products that are created through a complex, energy-intensive process involving black crude oil that releases toxins into the air. Petroleum-based products are more likely to pose health risks than plant-based products.

pH A measure of acidity and alkalinity of a solution that is a number on a scale (from 0 to 14) on which a value of 7 represents neutrality. Lower numbers indicate increasing acidity, and higher numbers indicate increasing alkalinity. Each unit of change on the pH scale represents a tenfold change in acidity or alkalinity.

Phantom load The electricity used by TVs, coffeemakers, and other devices when they're turned off. Items draw power from the outlet, which is why a cell phone charger is warm when it's plugged in, even if the phone isn't connected. Also known as vampire power.

Photovoltaic (PV) Pertaining to the direct conversion of light into electricity. PV cells, or solar cells, are semiconductors that produce electrical energy when exposed to sunlight. PV energy generates electricity by absorbing light energy rather than burning fossil fuels, so it doesn't release any greenhouse gases.

Plant based Products that are created using natural ingredients derived from plants. Plant-based products are safer for the environment—and your health—than petroleum-based products.

PVC A common thermoplastic resin used in a wide variety of products, including spray bottles, flooring, and siding. PVC usually contains toxic chemicals called phthalates and should be avoided.

R-value A measurement of a product's resistance to heat loss. R-value is the inverse of U-factor. The higher the R-value, the better a material's (floors, walls, roofs, and so forth) insulation qualities.

Sustainability The ability to meet the needs of the present without compromising the ability of future generations to meet their needs. A sustainable process is one that can be maintained indefinitely without a negative impact on the environment.

Toxin A substance that can cause severe illness, poisoning, disease, or death when ingested, inhaled, or absorbed by the skin. Quantities and exposures necessary to cause these effects vary.

U-factor A measurement of the rate of heat transfer through a product. U-factor is the inverse of R-value. The lower the U-factor, the better a window, skylight, or door insulates.

Volatile organic compounds (VOCs) Chemicals containing carbon at a molecular level that easily form vapors and gases at room temperature. Many cleaning and building products emit VOCs, which can be harmful to people and the environment.

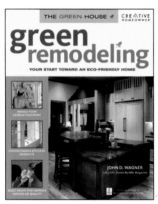
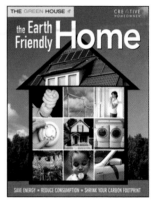